I Tell You All This Because...

Bonnie M. Colton

Homewood Books

ISBN 978-0-7414-2908-7 Paperback
ISBN 978-0-7414-9189-3 eBook

Published by:

INFINITY PUBLISHING

1094 New DeHaven Street, Suite 100
West Conshohocken, PA 19428-2713
Info@buybooksontheweb.com
www.buybooksontheweb.com
Toll-free (877) BUY BOOK
Local Phone (610) 941-9999
Fax (610) 941-9959

Printed in the United States of America

Published December 2012

Dedication

This book is dedicated, with appreciation,
to the memory of Miss Gladys Lodge,
my highschool biology teacher,
who listened patiently to my
head-in-the-clouds dream of becoming a writer,
and kindly gave me feet-on-the-ground advice;
to Gordie Allen, newspaper editor, for his
acceptance, encouragement and appreciation of
my early journalism efforts, especially my poetry;
to the late Livingston Lansing,
entrepreneur *extraordinaire*,
who believed in my projects and urged me onward;
and to my husband of 53 years,
Don Colton, who is, without question,
my biggest fan and most avid promoter.
I can never overestimate the positive effect
these individuals have had on my life.

--Bonnie M. Colton

Water Song

Black Creek cascades down rocky slopes
of the Western Adirondacks
on its way to a distant ocean.

Much like our lives, the stream
has its quiet stretches
and its boisterous rushes.

Nature, in all its infinite variety,
has secrets to whisper to us,
if only we will listen.

Cover photo by the author

Fore-Word

I was raised in a time when good stories frequently ended with a moral—a lesson about right conduct, or an idea to contemplate. As I came of age in the years following World War II, the mood of the nation was changing. There was a new feeling of freedom with the Depression and the War now history. Every wind carried a sense of adventure that grew to fill our expanding horizons.

We put the old behind us, even smiled patronizingly at the tried and true values that had marked the preceding years. One of the casualties of this new mindset was the moral tale, the story with an obvious lesson. The War taught us that life is both fragile and temporary, and that was more than we wanted to learn. We craved something to help us escape life's harsh realities—fun, instead of lessons.

Our literature became filled with "slice-of-life" stories that had ambience (we'd learned some French while in Europe), but often not much substance. Many were open-ended, with no satisfying wrap-up at all. They reflected the lives whose sense of future and predictability had changed profoundly.

We sang silly songs and told silly jokes. We wore silly fashions and danced silly dances. And we made fun of the moral tales that had marked our childhood.

I remember one such silly song. It was about a little man who went into a fancy restaurant. After he was seated, he checked his pocket and found he had only two halfpence. The menu showed little except one fish ball that he could afford. But when he told the waiter what he wanted, the waiter shouted the order, much to the embarrassment of the customer, who then whispered, "bread, sir, please." The waiter exclaimed loudly that the establishment did not serve bread with one fish ball. Mortified, the little man went outside and shot himself dead. The song ended with this fun-poking advice: "There is a moral to this all—don't order bread with one fishball." And everyone laughed. The need for moral advice had become passé.

I don't think I ever consciously realized how much I missed the helpful little lessons of my childhood, until long after I became a grandmother. Then, as I looked back over the clippings of essays I had written for my local newspaper, I noticed a recurring phrase in many of them. It said simply, "I tell you all this because...," followed by a pointed lesson or an invitation to think seriously about something in the story.

As I transferred old files from backup disks to my new computer, I sorted them by category in preparation for the books I knew I would one day write. A large number of these stories with a moral were filed in a folder labeled, "Because." A few of them appeared in my first book, *Walking a Roundabout Path*. But now it is time for them to shine on their own. I have changed or deleted the repetitious phrase, so that it doesn't become tiresome. But I hope you will notice its effects, and will accept the invitation to think beyond the surface of these stories. I believe you will find it time well spent.

Contents

Charlotte's Story

1996

Charlotte May Woodward was born March 11, 1892, at Germantown, in New York State's fertile Hudson River valley. Her parents, Frank and Alida Coons Woodward, lost three infant sons to croup and diphtheria, but lived to see four other children grow up. Mame was the eldest, followed by Charlotte, Fred and John.

Frank Woodward worked on a fruit farm where cherries, strawberries, raspberries, peaches and plums were shipped to New York City markets. It was on the fruit farm that Charlotte learned the responsibilities of work. She was taught at an early age how to pick and pack fruits with care, to prevent bruising.

When the girls were in their teens, Mame and Charlotte went to work for other families in Germantown. The woman Charlotte worked for was sometimes subject to seizures. Charlotte remembered once when they were out riding, the woman went into a "fit" and would have fallen off the seat except that Charlotte was able to hold her with one hand and guide the horse home with the other.

When she was about 19, Charlotte found a job in New York City, keeping house for two spinsters who were both school principals. Miss Johnson and Miss Roberts were very particular about how things were to be done, and taught Charlotte everything a good maid should know. During vacations she was given time off, and would ride the train home to visit her parents in Germantown.

On Sundays, she went to church and to a young adult group known as Christian Endeavor. It was there she met

William, a tall, serious looking young man who worked in Grand Central Station supervising the handling of mailbags for the Postal Service. He had grown up on a farm in Morristown, New York, on the banks of the St. Lawrence River. But his older brother went into farming with their father, and the farm was not big enough to support all of them. William moved to New York City when his application for a position with the Postal Service was accepted.

On October 20, 1917, Charlotte Woodward and William Colton were married at her sister Mame's home in Jersey City. They settled down to keep house in a little apartment on Seaman Avenue in New York City. Having learned excellent housekeeping skills from Miss Johnson and Miss Roberts, Charlotte almost lived up to William's expectations. But he was disappointed that she didn't iron his socks and underwear; his mother always had. Then, too, William was quite a bit taller and could see the dust on the chandelier, which she might have missed. As with all young couples, they had to make adjustments—things to laugh about in later years.

Their first child, Frances, was born on March 4, 1919, a tiny mite who didn't fare well. Charlotte couldn't nurse her, and nothing they tried seemed to agree with her except mother's milk. Another mother in the same apartment building had milk to spare, and for a while she nursed Frances. When that was no longer feasible, Charlotte took the baby to a doctor. There were no commercial baby formulas then. The doctor devised a formula made of beet, carrot and spinach juices. At last they had found something that worked and Frances began to gain.

Meanwhile, William was becoming restless. He said he was too light for heavy work and too heavy for light work. He longed to return to what he knew best—dairy farming. The family packed up and headed north to visit his parents in Morristown. They stayed for a month while William read

"For Sale" ads, talked to real estate agents, and looked at some farms which he considered too stony. His search took him to Port Leyden. The train went right through the little village and their was a hotel only a stone's throw from the railroad station. It would make a good place to stay temporarily while looking over the situation.

Rob Williams had rented the farm to others, but now was ready to sell. He showed William the old colonial house, the horse barn, dairy and hay barns and 50 acres of good farmland. A deal was made for the land and buildings, 18 bred heifers and a bull, a walking plow and disc, and a team, wagon and spreader, all for the post-war high price of $7,000. The seller would hold the mortgage.

On August 1, 1919, the Colton family rode up the hills out of Port Leyden to start the new adventure of life on a farm. As they came up Rugg Road, they saw smoke and flames in the vicinity of their new buildings. Dismayed, they urged their horse forward. Drawing closer, they found it was a barn fire on the hill above their place, and breathed a sigh of relief.

When William went up to see if there might be anything he could do, their new neighbor, John Bailey, stood looking at the ruins of a barn he had built for himself only five years before. William offered to board some of his cows while the barn was being rebuilt.

Charlotte was appalled at the condition of her new home. The roof leaked. Woodwork and windows were grimy. Wallpaper was stained and loose. There wasn't a door in the place that closed properly. Woodchucks and rabbits were camping in the cellar.

Disappointed, lonely and homesick, she sat in the drab emptiness of her new house and cried. She cried for the neighbor who had lost his barn; she cried for her baby, still pale and fragile; she cried for the unkempt condition of the house that was not yet a home; she cried for the unfamiliar, unfriendly future she imagined ahead. This was William's dream, not hers.

But Charlotte was not afraid of hard work. She was determined to make the best of it. William fixed the roof and Charlotte peeled sagging wallpaper. She scrubbed grimy woodwork and polished filmy windows. With a piece of broken glass she scraped layers of chipped paint off the big built-in china cabinet in the dining room until she found the original finish, then varnished it.

Together William and Charlotte hung new wallpaper to brighten up the rooms. She scrubbed the broad floorboards and he put filler in the cracks between them. While William got the barn into shape and tended the stock, Charlotte cooked and baked and rocked her baby and wrote letters and learned to endure.

The first winter was hard. The heifers that would start his herd wouldn't freshen until spring. No milk, no income. When the first mortgage payment came due, they had to borrow money just to pay the interest. A small flock of laying hens provided some food, and surplus eggs could be traded for other necessities at the store.

In the spring, Charlotte's brother sent her some strawberry, raspberry, currant and gooseberry plants. Busying herself with familiar fruits should help to ease her isolation. The berries thrived and soon she had plenty to eat and to make into jams and jellies. Eventually, the yields were so heavy she hired the Bailey boys to help her pick them.

Charlotte's days were filled with the busyness of farm life. She planted a large garden and spent hours tending her growing crops. She read to Frances. She made switchel for the men working in the hay fields. She canned vegetables from her garden. She learned to operate a hay fork which picked big bites of loose hay from the wagon and lifted them into the hay mow, where a helper would spread the hay with a pitchfork and pack it down tightly.

When Frances was four, she and her mother went by train to the funeral of Frank Woodward. For Charlotte, it was both joy and sorrow. She grieved for the father who was gone, but took comfort from being with her family for awhile.

Back home, Charlotte put renewed energy into her daily tasks, thankful for the time away, thankful for the big pullout bins in her pantry which kept sugar and flour for baking in easy reach, thankful for the gracefully curved staircase in the front hall which really was quite elegant, thankful for the front porch with its view across the valley to the distant mountains. Little by little her life was improving. She started a flower garden on the south slope of the lawn and added sunshine and fragrance to her rooms with lavish bouquets of peonies, iris, sweet Williams, lilies-of-the-valley, phlox, sweet peas, honeysuckle and French lilacs.

Eight years after they first came to the farm, a second child was born into the Colton family. They named him Donald, and he was destined to carry on the family farming tradition.

Charlotte saved her berry and egg money to buy curtains for the windows and new blankets, sheets and pillows. When she was satisfied her house was presentable, she invited paying guests to come for vacations. Many were people she had known in New York City. It was fashionable in those days to vacation in the country. And Charlotte's country home was the perfect setting for a relaxed week or more away from the city.

Frances soon grew up, married one of the Bailey boys and moved to Talcottville. A few years later, Donald also married, but stayed on the farm to raise his family and help his dad.

When Charlotte died in 1963, she left behind eleven grandchildren, a well kept home, a grieving husband and a life story of triumph over adversities.

Charlotte Colton was my mother-in-law and I learned much from her. I wish everyone reading this would collect and preserve such stories. See what lessons you can learn that will make your own life richer. Your interest in them will bless the individuals whose stories you preserve.

In Pursuit of Happiness

1995

"Happy New Year!" Everybody's saying it. It's such a cheerful, hopeful sound. And yet we wonder, what makes happiness?

If we listen to the TV ads for making dreams come true, we might think happiness is "asking all the men I ever loved, 'Who's sorry now?'" or "Taking the day off...and the next day...and the next...and the next," or getting new furniture, like the "dreamer" who says, "I've never liked my furniture...and I wouldn't have to any more." In other words, plenty of money equals happiness. But does it?

There is an ancient Chinese parable about a very rich man and his poor neighbor. The rich man observed that his poor neighbor seemed unhappy. When he inquired as to the reason, the poor man said, "If only I had enough money to do the things I'd like to do, then I could be happy."

The rich man, wanting his neighbor to be happy, gave him a large sum of money. The poor man thanked his friend profusely and hurried home to share the news with his wife.

The two of them set about earnestly to decide how they would spend their good fortune. They sat up very late that night discussing all the ways they might invest the money to reap a good return, for they wanted to pay back the kindness of their neighbor when they became rich themselves. For hours they talked, until they became exceedingly tired and finally fell exhausted into bed.

The following day, they resumed their deliberations. If they bought a fishing junk and some nets, and hired workers to help them, they might be successful fish merchants. If they spent the money on education, would they not be able to earn more? Shouldn't they buy a nicer home, then think of better ways to spend it after they lived in brighter surroundings?

All day long they pondered these and other ways to expand their wealth and thus become happy. Long after darkness came, they fell again, exhausted, into a restless sleep.

On the third day, they realized that they were in a perilous situation. If it became known they had so much money, who knows what robbers might scheme to steal into their house as they slept and kill them and run off with the treasure?

All day long they worried and fretted about the disasters which might befall them. That evening, the poor man went back to visit his neighbor. The rich man observed that his friend looked exceedingly tired and worried, and unhappier than he had looked before.

"What is troubling you, my friend?" he asked. "Did the money I gave you not make you happy?"

"Nay," replied the poor man nervously. "It has robbed me of sleep and taken away my peace of mind. I have no strength to do the daily tasks I must do." With this, he drew the parcel of money from his shirt and handed it back. "Take it," he said. "I have found that money cannot bring me happiness."

That night, the poor man and his wife slept long and peacefully, happy to have each other and a good night's rest.

"Happy New Year!" And I really mean that. But again I ask, what *makes* happiness? Money isn't the answer, or all the world's wealthy people would be happy. But they aren't.

Lack of money isn't the answer, either. Just ask anyone who lacks money, and they'll agree. That wasn't the point of the parable. The ingredient that brought happiness in the story was contentment. And contentment is an attitude that can be cultivated.

That doesn't necessarily mean being satisfied with the status quo. If we never strove for something better, something *more* in our lives, things could be pretty dull. But at least it's a clue to the source of happiness.

True happiness comes from within, not as a result of our possessions, circumstances, education or advantages, but as a result of our attitudes *about* all these realities.

When the poor man first went home with the gift from his neighbor, he was happy. Why? Because his attitude was one of excitement, anticipation, gratitude. He felt blessed.

After he returned the money and went home to sleep, he was again happy. Why? His attitude was one of relief, thankfulness, contentment. He felt blessed.

"Happy New Year!" YOU are blessed, too. Each one of us is blessed in so many ways. We are blessed with health and friends, shelter, food and clothing—great plenty, even for the poor among us, compared to many others in this world. The question is, what is our ATTITUDE toward those blessings?

Are we grateful for the ability to work? For the love of our family? For the respect of friends? For the trust of neighbors? For the opportunity to learn? For the hundreds of conveniences technology has placed in our homes and work places?

Are you happy? Do you want to be? Part of the secret is to make someone else happy. How? Not by giving them things. That might make them *seem* happy for a short time. But like the poor man in the story, it doesn't last. Instead, give them your friendship, respect, appreciation. Give them praise for accomplishments—even everyday ones. Give encouragement when they are struggling. Give them companionship. Give them a smile and a hug. You will be amazed at how happy it will make them. And you will be equally amazed at how happy it will make YOU!

"Happy New Year!"

New Year Resolutions

1996

Well, did you make your resolutions for the coming year yet? It's not too late you know, even though we're well into the second week of January. A year can start on any day you decide.

For example, on October 15, on my way home from visiting a cousin, I resolved to simplify my life and manage my time better. I didn't put it in just those words but that was the result I was looking for.

"I'm making a new year's resolution not to bother with any more sweepstakes entries. They eat up time and we never win anything anyway."

Don grinned at me with that, I'll-believe-it-when-I-see-it look. The new year was a long way off, after all. Privately, I decided to begin living out my new resolution the next day. I simply moved the new year, for that particular resolution, to October 16. It's easy. Anyone can do it. The results were spectacular. You should have seen Don's grin vanish when he saw me chucking Reader's Digest and Publishers Clearing House packets in the waste basket that very week. He was aghast at the possible millions I was throwing away.

Well, I figure it this way. If God wanted us to have five or ten million, or even $100,000, there's been ample time to make it happen. I'd been wasting time with sweepstakes entries for over twenty years. If I had saved, at compound interest, all the money I've thrown away on sweepstakes entry postage, I'd already have a sizeable jackpot.

Not only that, but if you read the fine print on the entry forms you'll notice the long lead time on some of those giveaways. "Entries must be postmarked no later than October 20, 1995," they warn, but the fine print says prizes will be awarded in January 1997, or maybe even July 1998. There's still time for us to strike it rich even if we never send any entries again. Of course I told Don he was free to fuss with them if he wanted to, but so far I haven't seen him doing it.

This new-year resolution has worked well so far. It really has saved me time and money and has helped unclutter my life. What could be simpler? Out of the mailbox and into the wastebasket. I've likely saved a whole book of postage stamps since I made this resolution almost three months ago.

In mid November, Don and I both made a new-year resolution. We'd been talking for a long time about our increasing lack of physical fitness. "We ought to walk more," we said, but with snow and ice in the way, the streets certainly aren't a very good choice this time of year.

We resolved to go to the fitness center and explore the benefits of some intentional fitness exercising. We started on November 17, and have been there at least three times a week ever since. We're both experiencing improved muscle tone, endurance and lung capacity. We both feel better, more energetic.

If I had resolved to lose twenty pounds in the next six weeks, I'd have given up by now. The scales are stuck right where they were when we started. Instead, I resolved to exercise three times a week for whatever benefits it might give. I know that muscle weighs more than fat, and I've been building muscle strength. Patience with the process is important in keeping any resolution. Patience with one's self is even more important.

I tell you all this to encourage you to make new-year resolutions, too. Just be sure your expectations are reasonable and will pay good dividends—in health, looks, self-esteem, friendships or maybe even increased income.

And remember, a resolution doesn't have to be for a whole year. Some people make successful resolutions for as little as one week, one day, or even one hour.

Look at it this way—a resolution is like fertilizer. You can grow houseplants without fertilizer but, if you want lush looking plants with beautiful blossoms, fertilizer helps it happen. It's just the same with life. You can live without making resolutions, but you can live a better, more satisfying life if you fine tune it with resolutions now and then. It's never too late to start.

On Making Resolutions

I resolve:
*to lose 25 lbs this month
*to send 5 letters each day
*to smile, no matter what
*to be the perfect wife
*to read a book every week
*to volunteer whenever asked
*to keep my house spotless all year.

Such new-year resolutions are a recipe for failure.
They are so unrealistic, no one could live them thru.
The Good Intentions Highway
fast becomes a brambled byway
full of stumbling blocks and pot holes
that are sure to conquer you.

Better far to make adjustments in a realistic manner,
challenging, but not demanding,
small steps toward a distant goal.
Each step is a celebration on the path to destination,
bringing added strength and courage,
making us more free and whole.

Regulations

1992

It seems just about every aspect of life is regulated today, some necessarily so. Child care is no exception. For instance, our state requires childcare providers to be registered if they are paid to care for more than two children who are unrelated to them.

But that's only a beginning. With unfortunate child care abuses making news, it was inevitable that regulations would become more detailed and stringent.

The problem is, regulations often are written by well-meaning people who have little concept of what is actually involved. And the people who *are* involved, sometimes find the rules impractical or even unworkable. Last fall, New York State issued proposed childcare regulations which were sent to known providers, social service agencies, child advocacy groups, etc., about 17,000 packets in all.

Tricia Kennison, Lowville, was one of the recipients. Tricia has operated a family day care in her home since 1987, and was the first in Lewis County to be certified for family day care. As she read the new rules through, Tricia jotted down comments, questions and suggestions which she sent to Albany for their consideration. She was one of about 500 who commented during the six-week response period provided. In January, revised regulations were mailed out as before. Again Tricia read them carefully and made more notes.

It is a common fallacy that one person cannot do much to influence bureaucracy. But I believe one person *can* make a difference. Tricia's remarks not only were read, as were all

the others, but she was invited to go to Albany this month, expenses paid, to take part in a roundtable discussion of the issues which had received the most criticism or questioning. This is the first time actual childcare providers have been invited to give their input in the regulation process.

Sponsored by the State Department of Social Services, Bureau of Early Childhood, the meeting was held at the Junior College of Albany, on March 4, from 11:00 a.m. to 4:00 p.m. Of the 36 people attending, Tricia was the only single-family childcare provider present. Several participants came to her before and after the meeting to tell her how impressed they were with her written comments and with her input to the discussion.

The regulations again are being revised and are expected to be reissued in permanent form later this year.

By now you may have wondered why I'm telling you all this. I think it is important for individuals to recognize their potential and not to *under*value their own opinions. The everyday citizen in the everyday circumstances of life has a better grasp on the realities of everyday living than the distant writers of regulations do. We're fortunate to have some rule makers who listen. So if you have something worthwhile to say, speak up!

Your voice counts

No person is unimportant.
Each has some gift to share--
A word of wisdom,
    A helping hand,
        A bit of wit,
            A prayer.

Be kind to yourself. Be patient.
And pull your share of the load.
Some day you'll find
    true peace of mind
And a song along life's road.

Baby Joey

1996

Let me tell you about Joey. His mother, loaded with alcohol and cocaine, stumbled into a big city hospital in premature labor. She was only 27 weeks into her pregnancy when Joey was born. He weighed under three pounds. His lungs were not fully developed and he was immediately placed on a ventilator in neonatal intensive care. He had to be fed through a tube and suctioned whenever his breathing rattled.

The day after Joey was born, his mother checked out of the hospital and never came back. A year later, with Joey still on life support, the state stepped in and took away his mother's parental rights. When asked about the baby's father, she had given them his name. The man hadn't even known about his son and was interested. In jail at the time, he had more problems of his own than he could cope with and certainly was not equipped to care for a special needs child. He was advised to "give the kid a break" and sign away his parental rights.

And so it was that little Joey became a ward of the state. It looked as if busy medical doctors and impersonal bureaucrats would be in charge of his doubtful future.

At this point, a nurse who had been working with him ever since his birth decided she would like to care for him at home. She was familiar with all his problems and necessary treatments, and was qualified to handle him. She had bonded with him as much as anyone had. Her husband agreed and was very supportive. They had been temporary, sometimes long-term, foster parents before in addition to raising their own.

Meanwhile, a nearby hospital had failed financially and been acquired by another hospital. Converted into a long-term care facility for head injury patients and others with debilitating problems, it was trying to get a large enough number of breathing-disorder patients to qualify for a full time respiratory therapist. The nurse-practitioner who was part of Joey's medical team, decided he should go there. She opposed the nurse's request, questioning the motives of the couple. Joey, unaware of the controversy, became an innocent pawn in a bureaucratic battle.

A hearing, held in a large conference room, seemed obviously designed to intimidate the prospective parents. There were some 40 experts present. Even though she had worked with Joey almost daily for over a year, the nurse saw only three people she knew in the room. The rest, she suspected, only knew what they'd been told by others with a social or political interest in the outcome.

The would-be parents were grilled by the experts about their motivation. Why would *anyone* want to adopt a severely handicapped, mixed-race child, they wanted to know. Taught not to become emotionally involved with patients, they simply couldn't understand that this couple loved the child and wanted to give him the best chance possible for a normal life. Their educated opinions ignored Joey's need for human warmth.

The nurse was not intimidated. She looked around at the experts and asked where they had been during all the previous month's of this child's life, and what qualified them to decide whether she and her husband were capable of raising Joey.

They finally agreed to a trial placement, but only if the couple lived with Joey for 72 hours in the hospital's family care center first to prove they could do it. The facility was only part of one hospital floor, very much like the other hospital floors, not a bit like conditions would be at home.

There were no kitchen facilities, no way of preparing meals. One had to go out for food while the other watched the baby.

There wasn't even a bed for them to sleep in. They took turns sleeping in a recliner and sitting up with Joey. Although he had not had constant monitoring in the hospital nursery, the authorities insisted he have it now. When her husband was at work and she had to go to the bathroom, the woman called a nurse in to watch the baby for a few minutes.

She was barely out of sight when the nurse called for her to come quickly. I'll be right back, she answered. I mean *now*, said the nurse. She ran back to find Joey had stopped breathing and looked gray. The substitute had no idea what to do. Quickly, the "mother" pulled out the clogged breathing tube and inserted a new one and Joey started breathing again. Obviously, placement in a medical facility was no guarantee for him either.

The family stayed at the required site only 24 hours. The father had a job to attend to, and the conditions were so far from homelike they couldn't possibly measure preparedness.

The nurse-practitioner, angry that her plans were foiled and her judgement questioned, let the couple know she would fight them every step of the way. Almost every day there was a specialist or caregiver in their home, documenting Joey's progress and reporting to the hospital staff.

Every week the foster parents were required to take Joey to the pediatrician to be weighed. And every month meant a trip to the hospital for lung function testing. There they had to wait for hours until the tests were analyzed before they could return home. There was so much hassle locally, they started driving to a neighboring city for follow-up care. Even with the extra travel, it took less time to complete the tests and be home again than it had locally. The pediatrician, on his own, went to the other city to explain Joey's history and needs.

The nurse-practitioner continued to monitor Joey's progress closely and filed a complaint charging child abuse when she found they weren't feeding him the formula she had prescribed. Now over two years of age, he was eating solid food three times a day and taking a supplement with more nutrients than the prescribed formula. The changes had been approved by the pediatrician.

When a state agency worker came to investigate the abuse charge, she found a social service worker there also. The mother was out of the room at the moment, and the caseworker remarked that it seemed to her the child was getting the best possible care. When the mother returned and found out what the complaint was, she sat down with them and showed how much more nutrition Joey was getting on the current regimen, and even though he was still below growth charts for his age, he was making steady gains.

The state worker, on hearing all the interference the family had to endure, told them to avoid the local lung unit and continue taking Joey elsewhere for monitoring. She also suggested their pediatrician write to the hospital telling what had been advised and why. The interference stopped.

Joey made great strides in overcoming some of his initial problems and his foster parents officially applied for adoption in September, 1995. They were approved, but bureaucratic wheels turn slowly. The paperwork is stalled on the desk of some official who probably knows nothing about the situation. Meanwhile, the state continues to pay the foster parents for his care, an expense the taxpayers could be spared if the system functioned efficiently.

Joey is four years old now. He has been off the ventilator for a long time and goes to nursery school daily. He still has inhalation therapy three or four times a day, administered by his foster mother. He is a cheerful and helpful child, but still has speech and coordination problems. These are minor compared to the likelihood that he would not have survived at all in the impersonal surroundings of a long-term care facility.

I tell you this to emphasize, once again, the immeasurable value of human touch and the life giving power of love. We need to guard these treasures from bureaucratic bungling and political maneuvering. Joey is a "grandchild" of ours and I just wanted to share his story with you.

Women's Rights

1995

Albany, New York. February 8, 1861—Elizabeth Cady Stanton appeared before a special session of the New York State Senate to plead for a change in the state's divorce laws. She wanted them to add willful desertion and cruelty as grounds for divorce. At that time, adultery (provable) was the only legal reason for divorce in the state.

The Senate, not inclined to let a mere hysterical female tell them their business, refused to yield to her entreaties. In gross negligence of the needs of thousands of its powerless citizens, the state government continued its medieval view of women as chattel, not allowing them legal escape from cruelty until 1966!

I went to our Collier's Encyclopedia, published in 1962, to do some research on Elizabeth Cady Stanton. She wasn't even mentioned. I checked the Collier's 1966 Yearbook and found no comment about New York State's divorce law change. I did find three items listed in the index under "Women's Affairs".

One concerned the slightly relaxing strictures on married women in Portugal. One was in the section on radio broadcasting. It mentioned, patronizingly, that "There were three all-girl stations." My dictionary, by the way, defines "girl" as an immature human female. I'm sure that's the way the largely masculine worlds of broadcasting and encyclopedia publishing viewed them.

The third reference to "Women's Affairs" directed me to one Mary Wells, found in the "Personalities of the Year" section. She was a high-powered advertising executive who left the firm where she worked, took some other employees and clients with her and established her own very successful firm. Curiously, she was the only woman from that section listed under "Women's Affairs".

Other females highlighted as 1966 personalities of the year were sex education proponent Mary Calderone, Oscar winning actress Julie Christie, world champion figure skater Peggy Fleming, Indian Prime Minister Indira Ghandi, British fashion designer Mary Quant and Alabama Governor Lurleen Wallace. One can only wonder why they weren't also listed in the index under "Women's Affairs", or why Mary Wells was singled out for that dubious distinction.

I remember the beginnings of the post-war feminist movement. It had been stirring behind the scenes before I became aware of it and was particularly active in the main line churches. I attended a meeting of the Utica Presbyterial in the late 50s or early 60s, in which the speaker belittled the designation of the women's program arm of the church as "Presbyterial." She said presbyterial was, by structure and intent, only an adjective, something of peripheral importance.

Big deal, I thought. What's all the fuss about? After all, our language would be pretty colorless without adjectives, wouldn't it? Likewise, the life of the church would be tasteless and dull without the energies and enthusiasms of its women. I thought the name presbyterial was very appropriate. Certainly it was preferable to the unwieldy "United Presbyterian Women of Utica Presbytery", the designation which now exists.

I tell you all these things because I believe if we get caught up in this kind of controversy we miss the whole point. All these arguments grow from social expectations of gender roles, which is only a peripheral issue. The central question is: How should we treat each other so that society will best be served and so that each individual will have the chance to reach optimum potential?

The answer is obvious. And simple. It was printed on the wooden ruler I used in second grade: "Do unto others as you would have others do unto you."

Living the Golden Rule

Imagine for a moment what it means
To co-exist within the Golden Rule,
To make allowances for others' flaws,
Knowing *we* need understanding, too.

Imagine how a day in class would seem
If all the students strove to do their best,
And if the teachers spoke encouragement
And treated each child as an honored guest.

Imagine how the family would improve
If no one griped or tattled or complained,
If all were thoughtful, patient, helpful, kind,
And everyone could share in blessings gained.

I think I'd like to live in such a world,
Where folks weren't judged by fame or intellect,
Nor by their social standing nor their wealth—
A world where *all* are treated with respect.

The Golden Rule, as it appeared on my wooden ruler in the second grade, said:
Do unto others as you would have others do unto you.

I restate it here for a new generation of hearers:
Treat other people the way you would want to be treated if you were in their circumstances.

Almost every religion in the world has its own version of the same principle. And yet it is not a religious principle; it is a human relations principle. Give it some serious thought, my friend, then put it into practice if you haven't so far. And may much good come to you as a result.

Rich or Poor?

1992

I often marvel that there are so many people who have very little memory of their early childhood. Some of my most pleasant recollections come from my pre-school years.

My parents were avid readers and always read bedtime stories to us. We had a large book illustrated with comical, fascinating, beautiful black-and-white drawings. It was called simply 365 Bedtime Stories. That meant if it lasted all year, we could hear only one story each night. But some of them were so short, we'd beg for more or ask to hear old favorites a second or third time.

Sometimes they would tell us a story instead of reading. Or one of them would recite a narrative poem. Recitations were a popular form of entertainment in those days, and each of our parents knew several good ones. Here was a favorite:

"Wynken, Blynken and Nod one night
Sailed off in a wooden shoe,
Out on a river of crystal light
Into a sea of dew...

"Wynken and Blynken were two little eyes
And Nod was a little head,
And the wooden shoe that sailed the sea
Was a wee one's trundle bed."

There was more, but I don't remember it all. I just remember it was soothing and quieting to listen to as our own little heads nodded off into a sea of dreams. We were loved. And we knew we were. The years have shown me how immensely important that was to my sense of self and my understanding of life.

In the morning there were chores to be done. We had one cow that Daddy milked each day. I didn't go to the barn with him, but waited for the fresh, warm milk to eat on my oatmeal. There was no refrigerator and no icebox in our house. A pitcher of milk was kept cool in a pan of clear cold well water.

Excess milk was poured into large milk pans and placed on the pantry shelf to lobber. Then Mother would skim the cream off and make butter in a small hand-cranked churn.

The sour milk in the bottom of the pan was used in baking or to make cottage cheese.

In summer when the weather was nice, Daddy would set the wash tubs up on sawhorses in the back yard so Mother could do the laundry out in the fresh air. Water was drawn up by the bucketful from the well, carried into the house and poured into the big copper boiler on the woodstove to heat. Then they carried pails of hot water out to the tubs in the yard and Mother went to work.

Sometimes she let me help her. She scrubbed sheets and shirts on the big scrub board and I scrubbed socks and hankies on the little scrub board. And we'd play word games as we worked. One of our favorites was "pairs". I'd say Adam; she'd say Eve. She'd say knife; I'd say fork. She'd say Mother; I'd say Daddy. I'd say lightning; she'd say thunder. And so it went— work and play and learn and love—all in one.

Saturday night was bath night. Again, water was heated in the big boiler. We had no bathroom, so the washtub was set on the floor in front of the kitchen stove where it was nice and warm. On really cold nights they'd leave the oven door open so we didn't get chilled, and bathtime went quickly.

But on warmer nights we'd linger and play. I remember Daddy taking a big dipper and pouring water over me like a summer rain shower. Then Mother would rub me all over with soap and Daddy would use the dipper again to rinse the soap off. I didn't believe it when he told me he could pour water into my shoulder and make it come out at my fingers. I watched in amazement as the water ran "in" my shoulder and—sure enough—"out" my finger tips! He certainly knew how to do magic, at least in my young mind he did.

There was another time his magic came in really handy. I was sitting on the side porch in the sun, barefoot, when a bug landed on top of my foot and stung me. It hurt like fire and a yellow circle spread on my skin where the bug had been. Daddy quickly mixed a few drops of water with the dust from the yard and made a little mud pack to cover the yellow spot. He said the mud would draw the pain right out in just a few minutes, and he held my hand and helped me bear the hurt. In almost no time the pain subsided and I wore that precious mud pack till it dried up and crumbled off

We often went for nature walks together on the Coffins Mills Road. My older brother David and I ran ahead, hand in hand, then waited for Mother and Daddy to catch up. Daddy would be carrying our little brother Larry Jim on his shoulders, and Mother cradled Dottie Jo in her arms.

We learned the different kinds of trees and wildflowers that grew along the road. We picked wintergreen leaves and chewed on them. And when we came home, we'd get Mother's nature books off the shelf and look at the colored pictures to identify the butterflies we had seen.

We were so happy I never even realized we were poor. By today's standards, we lived way below the poverty level. We had no electricity, no refrigeration, no indoor plumbing, no car, no telephone, no television, no washing machine, no clothes dryer, no hair dryer, no job, no welfare check, no food stamps, no Medicaid, no heating assistance, no WIC program. But we had each other and we had the "big three"--faith, hope and love.

Today's "poor" have most of the things we didn't have. But they still think they're poor. We were rich by comparison because we had what money couldn't buy. It's a matter of perspective and expectations. As someone has so aptly said, "Happiness is wanting what you have, not having what you want."

So I will continue to value the precious memories of a rich and happy childhood, and the lessons that were a natural part of growing up.

Childhood Memories

A homemade sandbox was hours of fun,
And a rope and a board and a tree
Made the perfect swing on a summer's day
For my brother David and me.

The hill out back invited a ride
Over the winter's snow.
And springtime walks in the sunny woods
Showed us where adder's-tongues grow.

The song of the robin calling for rain,
And the taste of cowslip greens,
And the golden smile of the dandelion
All colored my childhood scenes.

And I tell you all this
　　for I'm sure it's true—
That when families love and share,
Even though worldly goods are few,
There are riches beyond compare!

BESS

1995

The title was intriguing—"A Woman of Independent Means"—and I watched the miniseries with interest. Screenwriter Chris Myers did an excellent job turning a book, which was essentially just a long series of letters, into a compelling dramatic presentation.

Bess, the central character and letter writer, started with a note to a fourth grade classmate and expanded her horizons as life progressed. The story covered seven decades of her life, with letters to her best friend Totsie, her father and his second wife, her husband when he was away on business, her sister-in-law and her mother-in-law, and the man whose car had been in the wrong place when Bess's small daughter darted out into the street.

Bess, played by Sally Field, was an attractive only child of wealthy parents. Her husband was, also. The combination was less than idyllic because each was self centered. Unfortunately, a good many marriages start that way. Bess submerged herself in the good little wife role so completely that she actually thought her husband adored her. It was more than obvious to the viewer, however, that he had little inclination to be a family man. His business meant everything to him. The three children were raised mostly by Bess and the hired servants.

Tragedy dogged Bess's life as she attended funeral after funeral of people near and dear to her. Although she handled the suffering staunchly, on the outside, it began to work a subtle change within her that pushed people away. She wouldn't let new people close, wouldn't let herself treasure them, because she wanted to avoid the pain of eventually losing them.

But Bess found there is more than one way of losing loved ones. She lost her two surviving children to college and society and other interests. They ignored her letters, her invitations to holiday dinners, her efforts to steer their lives the way she thought they ought to go. She felt so out of control from the loss of mother, husband and one son, that she tried ever harder to control and protect those she had left.

The "woman of independent means" referred to inherited money and good investments which paid off well financially. Bess was definitely not independent emotionally; she constantly doted over husband, children, father. She was not independent socially; she was anxious to join the "in" groups such as the Shakespeare Club.

And Bess, although she liked to think she was a free spirit, was actually a slave to fashion, to adventure, to anything that would take her mind off her bitter sadness.

She ended up a pitiful little wizened old woman, pruning her rose bushes, the only thing left, over which she could exercise control.

I tell you all this because I'm convinced we need to be careful about *how* we let life affect us. Everyone's life holds heartache, sooner or later. It is a reality we cannot avoid. But we can choose how we will cope with it. Bess turned inward and her capacity to love was gradually replaced by the need to control. Not only did her body become shriveled, so did her soul.

I have learned, the hard way, that the best way to handle my own pain is to put it in God's hands and leave it there. Bess nursed her pain and kept it alive. I've found it more effective to concentrate on becoming aware of the pains and problems of others and offering encouragement and help when appropriate. Being available to other hurting individuals is a quiet, steady way to let healing into our own lives.

Seeking Happiness

Happiness is like a carrot
Dangled on a string before us,
Urging onward, ever onward
To the hope of finally reaching
What our hearts are truly seeking.

So we strive for fame and riches,
Thinking they will make us happy.
But they only disappoint us,
Make us anxious and defensive,
Make us long for something better.

Let me share with you a secret—
Happiness, when chased, escapes us.
No amount of striving wins it.
No amount of wealth can buy it.
No amount of wishing woos it.

If we truly would be happy,
We must cease our striving for it.
When we give our lives to others,
Give our all to make *them* happy,
Happiness, at last, will find US.

* * * * *

"Being available to other hurting individuals is a quiet, steady way to let healing into our own lives."—BMC

Changing of the Seasons

1993

Relief is spelled T-A-X-E-S D-O-N-E !! I double checked all the figures, photocopied forms to send with the State return, stapled papers together in proper attachment sequence, applied stamps and sealed bulky envelopes. Our check is on its way to the IRS. Whew! I feel like a marathon runner who just crossed the finish line.

I still think the IRS should hire English teachers or journalists to write instructions instead of lawyers and accountants. How much easier it would be for us, the daring souls who fill out our own tax forms.

Now it's time to do some serious desk cleaning, fold up the extra table I needed to hold the piles of paperwork, turn on the computer, and visit with you for awhile. Now *that's* a change of pace I can live with.

Snow is falling again. Winter is making a great bluster of a last stand before giving way to the inevitability of spring. We've seen the woodchuck holes, brown around the entrances, with tracks going here and there. Our conservation officer tells us the males come out first. They travel from burrow to burrow, fulfilling nature's new-life urge, then go back home and sleep for another month or so.

Squirrels, which haven't been around our yard as much as usual this winter, are out romping, scooting across the snow and spiraling up the trees in a dead-run game of tag. The cat is restless, wanting to get outdoors to explore, but just as eager to get back inside where it's warm and dry.

The canary is pulling his feathers out by the beakful, getting ready to sport a fresh coat of plumage. Daylight

creeps in through the windows a little earlier each day, tugs at my eyelids and whispers in my ears that it's time to get up. Even church pews are fuller as the early "snowbirds" come back from Florida.

At the hospital, a glass-walled corridor borders a bit of outdoors where an exit used to be. In that unexpected garden, flower buds are pushing their heads up at the edges of receding snow. Drifts still brush the bottom rail of our backyard fence, but around the tree trunks snow shrinks away, a sign the sap is beginning to flow.

The magic comes so softly, even in the midst of a March blizzard. Spring unfolds with quiet strength, pushing back the noisy winds and biting cold to make room for the northbound sun to warm the land.

The human spirit is like spring. It may seem to lie in chains of darkness, overcome by harsh realities and obstacles that rise, snowdrift-like, above its head. But underneath, like dormant crocus bulbs, the human spirit stirs to life. Quickened by an urge that will not be denied, it warms the soil around it and pushes upward, slowly, steadily, through layers of cold adversity, to bloom at last in sunlight and in beauty!

In early December, a son fell and partially crushed a vertebra in his back. At first he was told he'd probably be hospitalized for about 12 weeks. But he was at home in less than a week, wearing a brace until it became too much of a bother. In February, he went back to work full time!

When she was pregnant for her first child, a daughter fell on the ice. No one was around to help her as she struggled painfully to her feet and made her way into the house. The doctor told her she had cracked her pubic bone. There was a lot of pain and discomfort because the stress of pregnancy prevented the bone from healing. But she overcame that adversity. She now has grown children, and is stronger for having learned to endure.

A friend was psychologically battered by her husband. He finally abandoned her, leaving her to fend for herself and two babies. Reluctantly she applied for public assistance, but did all she could for herself. Eventually she remarried. Her babies, now teenagers, have a real father at last, not an elusive, undependable one. And the whole family is happy together.

Another neighbor sustained a disabling injury at work. Time eased the pain, but didn't cure the problem. Going back to her former job was out of the question. A winter of depression gripped her. Then a new opportunity opened up, one which she hadn't even considered before. Today she is happy in a new career, earning more than she did before, both in money and in job satisfaction.

Another neighbor was nearly killed when the machine he was operating went berserk. Mangled and in pain, he spent long days unable to work. Several unemployed friends came and cut his winter's wood for him. Instead of giving in to despair, he helped his friends in return with needed cash to feed their families.

Another friend had a very successful career in management. She was making excellent money and had enviable perks. But her company was pushing her into areas where she felt morally uncomfortable. She quit. Then hard times hit the business her husband was in, and she felt useless for not helping. She became severely depressed, making the family situation even worse. Her whole existence seemed encased in a glacier of hopelessness. The melting of that glacier took months, but today she is healthy and busy, earning a good living, and finding fulfillment in a new line of work.

A young couple's world almost fell apart when their new baby was hospitalized with a deadly disease. The doctors said the baby probably wouldn't make it, and if it did survive, would in all likelihood be profoundly retarded and possibly even blind and deaf. They refused to give up hope, but fought the establishment for every bit of help they could get for that baby. Today they have a healthy, happy child. And, although there are still some problems to overcome, slow steady progress is being made. The doctors have been astounded time and again by the accomplishments they thought could never happen.

I tell you all this because I see a real parallel between the coming of spring and the coming-into-its-own of the human spirit. When we are faced with the difficulties and discouragements that strike our lives like winter storms, we can take courage from knowing that no season lasts forever. Circumstances do change. We can overcome the snowdrifts of trouble that try to bury us.

Just Around the Corner

Do not despair, tho' winter may seem long.
The spring WILL come, and with it, joyful song!
The trials of life will melt and disappear.
Awake. Stretch up. And welcome spring this year.

Child Abuse

1993

"Nearly all prison inmates were abused as children." Don heard this last week on a Canadian radio station. The talk show's guest had worked for years studying the psychology of imprisoned criminals, and had yet to find any who had *not* been abused.

He also shared this fact: Inmates who participated in group therapy sessions to work out their feelings about childhood abuse, showed a much lower recidivism rate than those who didn't get help.

Not all abused children become criminals, of course. But relatively few may experience the healing help of group therapy sessions.

Writer Eric Mortenson tells the story of a man who stood on a street corner, day after day, holding a hand lettered sign: HELP STOP CHILD ABUSE. Some made fun of him. But when cars stopped for the traffic light, he'd often step off the curb and hand out leaflets he had prepared. They were written in capital letters, a mute testimony to his strong feelings on the subject.

I WAS ABUSE WITH MY TWIN SISTER FOR 20 YEARS. I WAS SAT ON HOT STOVE...EAT MY OWN VOMIT...TIED UP AND BEATEN WITH A STICK ...EAT MANY BARS OF SOAP...STAND IN SNOW WITHOUT SHOES.

PLEASE HEAR MY CRY FOR HELP TO HELP STOP CHILD ABUSE.

These are only brief excerpts. There was much more, and much worse written in his leaflets. The point is, this man survived and did NOT become a criminal. He used his misfortune to help save others from a similar fate. He must have had an innate sense of his own self worth. Many abused children have had their self esteem battered as well as their bodies and minds.

Children are the building materials society is given to use in creating the future. You cannot build a strong house using splintered beams and cracked blocks and frayed wiring. And we can't build a strong society when fractured families are giving us children with splintered personalities, cracked self-images and frayed nerves.

Neglect, willful or ignorant, is a far more subtle form of abuse. Last Tuesday, the CBS Evening News carried a segment about the many children in this country who start kindergarten totally unprepared for learning. Their parents never read to them or do structured activities. Many of these children have no acquaintance with the alphabet, have never visited a museum or done other learning readiness activities.

One school started a visiting teacher program for these disadvantaged children. She found that the parents often were barely more than children themselves and had no idea how to be effective parents. They had never been read to, and had never had their own parents play learning games with them.

Somewhere along the line we have to address these basic-basic problems in our society. We throw money at poverty, expecting it to buy the necessary food and clothing. But money cannot alleviate the mental poverty that results from fetal alcohol syndrome. Money cannot lift the load of guilt and unworthiness growing in a child who is being sexually abused. Money cannot restore dignity to a child who has been verbally battered. And money cannot keep an abusive parent from abusing again and again.

We throw money at our educational system. But money cannot motivate a child to learn. Too many youngsters are put through the educational mill and come out functionally illiterate. So much attention and money are spent on an extensive sports program that the athletically talented few have some of their needs met, but the socially inept and psychologically damaged children too often find school just another breeding ground for personal failure.

Where are the teachers who focus on building self esteem? Where are the classes that major in promoting the *fun* of discovery and learning? Where is a curriculum to develop skills in self awareness, successful interpersonal relations, goal setting? What athletic event teaches children to be compassionate, forgiving, kind? What science lab gives insight into human nature?

I'm convinced that large centralized schools are not the best answer to our educational/social/moral needs. The average student can feel overwhelmed by the sheer volume of people and classes, teacher/parent expectations, required homework, and competition for recognition. Individuality and creativity are often mangled in the mad rush for excellence in math/science/sports.

Tom Skinner Associates is a Washington-based group tackling this complex educational shortfall at its roots.

Tom Skinner was a ghetto kid who grew into a tough gang leader, feared by hundreds. Then he experienced a total change of outlook and actions when he became a Christian. He quit the gang and grew to be a very persuasive preacher. But he remembered his roots, the abuse and neglect and poverty, the lack of education and the low self esteem which were part of the ghetto experience and which drove kids into gangs so they could BE somebody.

Several years ago he established a Learning Center in Newark, New Jersey, in a high crime/high poverty/high unemployment area. At first only a handful of kids came, out of curiosity, or because there was nothing to do at home. He began to teach them three basic things. He taught them math, language and social skills so they could function effectively in the world. He taught them a trade so they could be self supporting. And he taught them that God had a prior claim on them and expected them to deal fairly and honestly with others.

Hundreds of disadvantaged youngsters now attend after school and summer training sessions at the Learning Center, often improving three grade levels in just a few weeks under the challenge and discipline of Skinner's three-pronged approach.

Any mathematician can tell you that a formula won't work if you leave out a necessary component. Today's public schools, by government decree, have left out the critical component needed for effective education—God's prior claim! The challenge and discipline of moral responsibility is lacking, and the formula is not working.

Overflowing prisons and battered children bear evidence to what happens when God is left out of the formula for life. We need to learn from history. Study the individuals who helped make this country a respected world leader. In almost every case, you will find a person of faith, raised within a strong moral and ethical family tradition. Children still need that rock solid foundation.

Prior Claim

"Children," says the Good Book,
"Are a heritage from the Lord."
They are a gift,
    A responsibility,
        A challenge.
God's prior claim gives focus to this trust,
Enabling us to value what is given,
Empowering us to be both kind and just
Rewarding us with blessings sent from Heaven.

Cuddle

1995

"Nobody cuddles anymore," a friend remarked. My mind stopped in mid-conversation to ponder what she had said. Is it true that nobody cuddles anymore? Nobody? That's stretching the indictment a bit too far. But it may well be true that in general there is less cuddling in our society than there was in my childhood.

Before you ask what difference it makes, let me tell you about an experiment I heard of many years ago. It took place at a foundling hospital in New York City, where unwanted babies, or babies whose parents couldn't afford to keep them, were left. Babies were a low priority in the city's budget and the hospital was understaffed with overworked and underpaid women who scarcely had time to make the rounds of all the cribs doing minimal care.

The babies were bathed, changed and fed on schedule but they failed to thrive. Many simply lay there and died. The medical authorities were puzzled. There didn't seem to be any scientific reason why so many of these infants wound up in the morgue. One of the nurses suggested that volunteer grannies might be recruited to come in and hold and cuddle the babies, which the attendants did not have time to do. The experiment was tried and the death rate dropped dramatically.

Another story concerned a single family where the babies did not gain weight as expected. They were being fed properly, but they remained tiny and pale and listless. A study was made and it was found the father had a well developed sense of self esteem and was busy earning a living, paying almost no attention to the children because his upbringing had taught him that raising children was women's work.

The mother had been an orphan who had known only minimal care in her formative years. She had no idea what babies needed other than a bottle of formula several times a day and a diaper change now and then. Her time was divided between this sporadic care, a little housework, hours of TV, and playing with the dog—a carryover from the sparse comfort of her own childhood.

The mother became ill and for several months was unable to care for the children at all. They were sent to live with their father's mother where they promptly began to make normal weight gains and where they took on a healthy glow they never had at home.

Grandma bathed them and cuddled them, read to them, played games with them and fed them nourishing meals. In grandma's house they felt as if they belonged. They felt cherished. They felt worthwhile. They thrived.

I tell you all this because, if people don't cuddle anymore, as my friend observed, then we're in big trouble. Think about it. When was the last time someone cuddled *you*? How did it make you feel? Cared for? Cherished? Important? Contented? These are the very feelings we need to experience in order to develop a sense of self worth.

When I was a child TV hadn't been invented yet. I'm sure if we'd had one, I'd have parked myself in front of it by the hour because I was enthralled by movies from the time I first saw one. But now I'm glad we didn't have TV. Instead, Mother cuddled me and read to me and played games with me and taught me all sorts of interesting things about the world around me. I felt loved.

I honestly believe there is nothing more vital in the life of a child than love. And cuddling is a tangible expression of love understood and absorbed even by newborns.

"Billy" was such a child. Although both of his parents worked outside the home, Billy was left in the care of a loving sitter from the time he was only a few weeks old. There he was cuddled and cherished and talked to. There he grew into a sweet tempered child, eager to please, quick to learn, friendly. But he preferred the sitter's company to that of his parents, often rebelling against going home with them at day's end.

The parents judged his attachment to the sitter unhealthy. They pulled him up by the roots and sent him to another sitter without any preparation. They blamed Billy and sent him to his room if he cried. When he tried to do something to please them, they ignored him or scolded him. Billy became pale and withdrawn, a shadow of his former cheerful self. And his parents, both well-educated people, apparently think this is healthier than his attachment to the sitter who loved him.

Billy is no longer vibrant and outgoing. He suffers emotional abuse and neglect by well-meaning, well-educated parents who are ignorant of basic human needs. But that emotional abuse and neglect leave no visible bruises or scars. Child protective services cannot help. What will happen to Billy? What will happen to our society if, in fact, no one cuddles anymore?

We live in an area of the country where several Amish families began buying farms a few years ago. Some of their children have grown up, married, and started families of their own since then. It is a pleasure to watch their young children go about their work and play. A calm peacefulness surrounds them. Usually they are cheerful and helpful, in contrast to the bickering, teasing and competition one often sees in other families.

Don remarked about this to one of the older Amish mothers. She said she thought it was because they were rarely left to cry as babies, but would be picked up and cuddled at the first sign of fussiness.

We would do well to learn from their mothering skills.

Cuddle Song

Cuddle down, my tiny baby.
Rest your head in Mother's arm.
Do not fear unknown tomorrows,
She will keep you safe from harm.

Cuddle close while Daddy sings you
Some sweet gentle lullaby.
Little one, disturbed in dreaming,
You are loved—no need to cry.

Cuddle up on Mother's lap, child,
As she strokes your fevered brow.
Soon again you will be healthy
For she loves and soothes you now.

Cuddle when goodbyes are whispered
As the young ones leave the "nest",
Stepping out to brave the future,
Searching for the path that's best.

Cuddle friends in times of sorrow.
Wrap them close in love's embrace.
Let your tears together mingle,
Bringing strength, the pain to face.

Cuddle close a favored pillow
When life finds you all alone.
Bask in memories of loved ones
And the blessings you have known.

When your life at last is over
And with wing-ed feet you're shod,
You can fly at last to heaven,
Cuddled in the arms of God.

Frugality—A Lost Art?

1995

Let's talk about frugality. That's an old fashioned word rarely heard anymore. I suspect many high school graduates never heard it or, if they did, simply didn't bother to look up the meaning. Frugality: the ability to live economically with prudent handling of few resources. Frugal comes from the same root as fruitful, and originally meant productive.

Those of us who lived through the Great Depression of the 1930's, and there are many who remember the hardships of those years, are well acquainted with the ways of frugality. The oldsters used to say:

"Use it up. Wear it out. Make it do or do without." And that's exactly what we had to do to survive. An interesting by-product of this philosophy is the fact that we had no megadumps to leak into our water table, no noisy trash trucks filling the air with fumes and flies, no pristine wilderness dumped on by a careless, non-frugal society.

What happened to our "trash"? Well, to begin with, few people could afford the luxury of newspapers or magazines. Those who could, often shared their used reading matter with neighbors who in turn passed it on to others. When worn out, such paper products were simply used for starting fires in our woodstoves or, yes, as toilet paper in our outhouses. And we survived. Very well.

Plastics hadn't made their appearance yet, so there were no styrofoam meat trays or picnic cups to clog landfills. Meat was wrapped in wax paper by the butcher, for those who could afford meat, and the wrapping was burned in the cookstove. Camping and picnicking utensils were made of tin, aluminum or enamel ware and were easily washable and reusable.

There were no plastic bread wrappers or sandwich bags or freezer containers or plastic dinner plates and cups. Dinner wear was ironstone or other chinaware or enameled metal. There were very few freezers, mostly in stores, and frozen foods were packed in waxed cardboard containers—burnable. Bread came in cellophane or waxed paper, also burnable. Those who carried lunches always found their sandwiches neatly wrapped in waxed paper, frequently saved and reused.

Diapers were cloth. Washable. No disposables to glut landfills. When they wore out, they were used for cleaning rags until they were unusable, then burned in the cookstove. Clothing was passed down from one child to another, from one family to another. It was patched when torn, darned when worn. And when it finally came to the point where it couldn't be used anymore, the zippers and buttons were removed for use on other garments whose fasteners were broken or missing, or on new homemade clothing. The fabric itself was used for cleaning rags if appropriate, or sold to the junk dealer who in turn sold it to the paper mills for use in high quality, rag-content writing paper.

Soft drinks hadn't been invented. Folks drank iced tea or lemonade or switchel--a cooler made of vinegar, ginger, sugar and water. Beer could be purchased on tap at the pub, and wasn't even available yet in throw-away containers. Milk came in quart and pint glass bottles, washable and reusable. We simply set the clean bottles out on the porch at night and they would be replaced the next morning by bottles of farm fresh milk. With cream on top.

Let's see, what else clogs our landfills? O, yes. Used appliances--TV's (they didn't exist then), washers and dryers (our washer was a tub and scrub board and our dryer was a clothes line or, in bad weather, an in-house drying rack. We didn't have an electric mixer—got our exercise by stirring cookie dough with a big spoon. Our toast was made in a wire-frame "toaster" on the hot, flat surface of the cook stove, wiped clean with a rag after each meal. No toaster or mixer to go kaput and end up in a dump.

As for broken furniture, which was rare, it was simply repaired and put back into use. Scraps of wood and wire, a little glue and some nails or screws could do wonders. Furniture which couldn't be repaired still made good heat when burned.

Food was hard to come by and not much was wasted. In the barn behind our house we had a recycling machine which we referred to as the family cow. It not only gave us milk for drinking, cooking, butter and cheesemaking, it ate all our carrot and potato peels and garden trimmings. It's manure eventually went back on the garden to enrich it for another year's production. A very efficient setup. On rare occasions, mainly during hunting season, we had meat to eat. Bones and other table scraps went to the dog.

There was hardly a thing we couldn't use up, wear out, make do, or do without. Trash, as we know it today, simply didn't exist. Even tin cans were rare, and they rusted out and returned to the soil fairly quickly. Most canned food was canned at home in reusable glass jars. And since we didn't waste time with hours of TV, we had time to do all those things that needed to be done to maintain our frugal lifestyle.

I tell you all this because I think we need a paradigm shift in our societal attitude, a new-old look at how we can live without depending on the government to provide everything for us. The virtues we used to value—hard work, self reliance, responsibility, initiative, inventiveness, frugality—have eroded over the years until there's hardly anything we don't expect the government to do for us.

Whether it's trash removal, child care, health concerns, education, entertainment, care of the aged and handicapped, highway maintenance, a helping hand for the less fortunate, or safety and affordability of our food supply, we expect the government to help take care of it for us. Then we wonder why we literally have to spend months earning enough money just to pay our taxes each year.

Let's do something constructive about it. Let's resolve to practice frugality. Let's get our expectations back in line with our own personal level of resources and not expect government to do for us what we could and should be doing for ourselves.

I'm not suggesting a return to the lifestyle of the 30's, but every one of us could do more for ourselves and expect less of government than we do. Government, after all, is simply an expensive bureaucracy taking money out of our pockets and our neighbors' pockets, and re-distributing it. Inevitably, some sticks to fingers along the way.

Summary

Value work.
Don't shirk.
Use your head.
Nuff said.

Unexpected Events

March, 1999

Isn't life in the north country invigorating? It's like a good marriage, often unpredictable, always interesting. We can make educated guesses about what's next, but sometimes all our expertise is wrong and we are blessed with yet another surprise. One day will be unseasonably sunny and mild. The next morning we wake to find spring has played a trick on us. It has wrapped all our tree branches in giant puffs of white cotton and spread a lovely fresh blanket on the lawn.

It isn't so lovely in the driveway, of course. It is wet and heavy and not very easy to move. But that's the way life is, beautiful and sloppy, a wonderland and a squalling inconvenience.

At least it isn't boring. If we wanted predictability in our weather, we could move to Phoenix, or Seattle, depending on which kind of weather we'd like to see.

And if we wanted predictability in our relationships, we could be hermits and live our own neatly scheduled days. I can't imagine being content that way for very long. I may fuss over interruptions and sudden changes of plans, but they actually add spice to life. They also help to keep us from taking ourselves too seriously.

I saw a TV special about Yehudi Menuhin, a virtuoso with the violin, who died earlier this month. His whole life was one surprise after another, at least to those who watched his progress. He was only seven years old when he first performed on his violin in public. The event took place in

San Francisco and was critically acclaimed, with praise that equaled any given to adult violinists.

At 11, he played in Carnegie Hall and at 13, he played a concert in Berlin. It is reported that at that concert, Albert Einstein was so moved that he met the young performer backstage, gave him a big hug and said, "Now I know there is a God in heaven!" That was in the spring of 1929, not long before Hitler came to power. Menuhin, born of Russian Jewish parents, would have to avoid Berlin during the war years.

A native of the U.S.A., Menuhin turned his talents toward entertaining troops during World War II. It was during those years the child prodigy grew up. Well, almost. He grew up physically, but he refused to leave his childlike enthusiasms behind.

He married a professional dancer, someone who knew and appreciated good music. She adored him, but never quite got used to his mischievous sense of humor. Even in his older years, she chided him with a condescending smile about his actions. He once stood on his head and conducted an orchestra with his feet for the sheer pleasure of doing something unexpected.

He was still going strong, entertaining crowds with his exceptional musical talent, when he had to cancel a scheduled concert for health reasons. He was in Berlin again when his time ran out. He would have been 83 next month. Yehudi Menuhin was a man who believed in *living* life, not just letting it happen to him. If they have violins in heaven, I expect he is sharing his gift there, too.

I saw a man this morning on television who brought flowers home to his wife unexpectedly. When she asked what the occasion was, he told her he'd seen them thrown in a dumpster at the funeral home and figured someone else might just as well enjoy them. After this, he often checked the dumpster and brought flowers home if there were any discarded arrangements there.

The other day our daughter had a luncheon meeting to go to and her two young children were out of school for the day because of the snow storm. So she left them with me and we watched a movie together, an unexpected time of fun with grandchildren.

There is an interesting fable about the "Three Princes of Serendip", who had an unusually eventful existence. Everywhere they went, good fortune seemed to find them. The word serendipity grew out of that tale and describes the life of people who seem almost to stumble into fortunate situations or make fascinating discoveries in the course of their everyday work or travels.

I have my own theory about serendipity. It is not just a literary invention; it is a frame of mind, an attitude of joy and expectancy, curiosity and excitement. If we spend our lives looking at the messy mud puddles that beset our path, we'll miss the serendipity of a double rainbow! We have to learn to focus more on possibilities and less on problems.

In last week's column, "This Side of 60", Marie Snider reminded us of the Delaney sisters, Sadie and Bessie. If you've never read their books, it is certainly worth your time just to see how much human beings can do when they have the right frame of mind. They were born into a large family with low-income parents who encouraged their children to excel. All the children became well educated contributing members of society, many of them professionals. Sadie was a teacher and Bessie was a dentist, an unusual occupation for a woman in the early years of the 20th century.

After retirement, the two sisters and their mother shared a home away from the rush of city life. But they weren't about to vegetate. Sadie insisted they be as professional about growing older as they had been about handling their careers. She noted that babies are flexible and limber and that old people usually became quite stiff. Determined to meet age with grace and good health, she instituted a daily habit of stretching and bending exercises that would keep all three women limber far beyond the time most folks take to their rocking chairs.

The sisters were both past 100 when a young writer came to help them put their life story on paper. It was fascinating to read and was illustrated with photographs of their parents and siblings. A picture of Sadie, all wrapped up in her exercise routine, was there, too. Actually her ankle was wrapped around the back of her neck. I believe she was 104 at the time. She lived to be 109, and relished the storehouse of good memories she had acquired. She didn't do all these things by whining and complaining and asking for handouts when she could very well do things for herself, even if it wasn't always easy.

I tell you all this because I think attitude has everything to do with how satisfactorily we live our lives.

Are we determined to look for the best in every situation?

Do we go out of our way to see the good in other people and to encourage it?

Can we honestly say we greet each new day with joyful expectancy?

Do we set high goals and work toward them with faithful determination?

Do we welcome variety and give thanks for unexpected blessings? If we do, our minds and hearts will remain young even if our bodies grow old. It's worth giving some thought.

"Focus on mud puddles, and you'll miss the rainbows!" – BMC

Celebrating Mothers' Day

May 1995

"I love you, Mother," said little John.
Then, forgetting his work, his cap went on
and he was off to the garden swing,
leaving his mother the wood to bring.

"I love you, Mother," said little Nell.
"I love you better than tongue can tell."
Then she teased and pouted full half the day
Till Mother rejoiced when she went to play.

"I love you, Mother," said little Fan.
"Today I'll help you all I can."
So she rocked the baby till it fell asleep.
Then stepping softly, she got the broom,
swept the floor and dusted the room.
Busy and happy all day was she,
cheerful and helpful as child could be.

"I love you, Mother," at night they said,
three little children going to bed.
I wonder how their mother guessed
which of them really loved her the best?

* * * * *

My mother used to tell this rhyme to us when we were small. I have no idea who wrote it, but whoever did should be thanked. That rhyme helped make me a cheerful and helpful child who truly loved her mother. I'm glad for those memories. They help to ease the loss I still feel after almost 20 years without her.

I'd like to tell you a little more about my mother. In the first book of this series, *Walking a Roundabout Path*, I told you that when my mother was five, her father and sister both died of tuberculosis. This was in 1905, long before Social Security benefits for widows and children.

Her mother did what many widows did in those days. She took in boarders. One of them Mother used to tell me about was named Miss Hoyle. Her photograph shows her frail and elderly with a genteel look about her. She was a spinster with only one brother. He traveled in Europe and once sent Miss Hoyle a special gift from there, an exquisite black Chantilly Lace shawl. Because there were no heirs, my mother inherited the shawl and, decades later, passed it on to me.

Another boarder at Jessie Seaman's house was a man named Jerry Madden. Mr. Madden was a pattern maker for the Columbian Rope Company in Auburn. This means he made the patterns from which they built the rope-making machines. It was a very responsible position. Eventually Mr. Madden, a bachelor or widower, asked Jessie Seaman to be his wife and she consented. They had no children except for young Marjorie.

Now Marjorie was an artist at heart. By her teens she was making remarkable copies of paintings by famous artists. I remember an oil painting she did of one horse's head, copied from the famous painting, "Horse Fair", by Rosa Bonheur. My youngest brother has that one. Another one, of a lighthouse on a rocky New England coast, now graces the wall in our youngest daughter's house.

Marjorie had often talked about becoming a commercial artist. She would have made an excellent one. But. When she was nearing high school graduation, she asked her mother for details on how she could get into art school to prepare for her career.

"Why, that's nonsense," she was told. "We don't have money for such frivolous things. You'll be a teacher, of course."

Crestfallen, Marjorie did as she was told and was enrolled in Oswego Normal School for its two-year teacher training class. She did well despite her severe disappointment, and eventually was employed as teacher for a one-room school somewhere near Auburn. She never really liked it, but she did like the children and took pictures of them which she often let us look at when we were growing up.

At 29, Marjorie married Charles Myers. They lived near her mother for a short time until after Jessie died and my older brother, David was born. Then the Myers family migrated to Oswegatchie, one of the many hamlets that dot the western Adirondacks. It was there I first saw the light of day. My parents had four children before their marriage ended in divorce. Mother then married Albert Stevens and had two more sons.

Needless to say, she never forgot her love for painting. But it was put on hold for many, many years. We moved to Lowville in the fall of 1945, and in the spring of 1946, Mother found work in the kitchen at Lewis County General Hospital. She worked there for twelve years before a stroke ended her working career.

Fortunately, she was not paralyzed. But the stroke left her with aphasia, the loss of almost all her memory of words. For months she could not read anything and make sense of it. She could not remember the names of even common objects. The only names she knew were her own and those of her children. Her children-in-law and her grandchildren looked familiar to her, but she couldn't tell you who they were. It was a lonely and frustrating time for her. She stayed with me for a few weeks until she began to recover some of her language ability, but my young and growing family was too much for her nerves. As soon as she could, she returned to her home in Lowville.

Eventually she moved to the new Extended Care Facility at Lewis County General Hospital. Here she found a happiness she had not known for years. The activity department had a corner where she could set up her easel and paint! Almost all her spending money went to buy paints, brushes and canvas boards. She made painting after painting and freely gave them away to neighbors, relatives and childhood friends with whom she had re-established contact. A large painting of Cranberry Lake still hangs in one of the dining rooms at the nursing home, a silent tribute to an artist fulfilled at last.

I tell you all this because Mothers Day is coming and I'd like to urge each of you to do what I have done here. Write the memories of your mother's life. If she is still alive, so much the better. You can ask her a million questions to fill in the blanks in your knowledge. Don't put it off until she's not here to ask.

Stories

Each person has a story just waiting to be told,
A fascinating, lively tale all full of teller's gold.
And some may tell of triumphs, while others speak of pain,
Or disappointments banished like sunshine after rain.

Now, those who choose to listen with keen, attentive ear
Will gather up a treasure to bless them year by year.
And those who share their story with some inquiring guest
Will see themselves thru new eyes, and so be doubly blessed.

Spring in the Adirondacks

May 1992

"There seems to be a madness in the cities, a frenzy in the struggling crowds. I am thankful for the peacefulness and comparative isolation of country life. This is a happiness which we ought to realize and enjoy." –Laura Ingalls Wilder, 1919

I can feel a kinship with Laura when it comes to city versus country living. Don and I are not crowd oriented. We like being with people in small groups but wouldn't do at all well in the crush of city life. When we take trips or mini vacations, we usually schedule them during the off season so we can enjoy the richness of nature unhampered by milling sightseers.

We drove through the Adirondacks on a sunny spring afternoon between the snowmobile and skiing enthusiasts and the summer sun seekers. I carried a notebook with me and jotted in it some of the sights and sounds along the way to share with you.

The temperature was around seventy, so the windows were rolled down—an open invitation to the black flies. Fortunately, they weren't interested in feeding—just exploring. Along the open highway they hit the windshield like rain showers, except they left it dirty instead of clean.

At the busy corner in Old Forge a trio sat on a bench by the sidewalk practicing music together. A fiddler sat on one end of the bench and a guitarist on the other, their instrument cases on the grass by their feet. Between them, a young woman with an autoharp and a high, clear voice was singing words I couldn't catch as we passed by. How delightful! And how different from the curb-to-curb relaxation seekers who'll be there in six weeks or so, trying to shift gears from the rush of their busy schedules to the serenity of mountain air and scenery.

The day was perfect with a light blue cloudless sky. Carefree bird songs filled the air. Laughter floated from open windows. Newly painted highway lines added their cheery gold to the color patterns of the mountains, trees and flowers.

From hamlet to hamlet we played leapfrog with delivery trucks—a white van sporting a potato chip company's logo, a bright yellow bread truck and a low-slung fire-engine-red tractor trailer loaded with soft drinks.

Between towns were the mirror-like lakes where white birch tripods seemed to stand. And here was a beaver meadow, acres of forest transformed to gray trees, decomposing in the encroaching marshland. And there was a hillside covered with small lacy-green tamarack trees stretching up. And along the road stood ancient gnarled pines wearing a winter coat of moss.

Village shops were hung with potted fuchsias, and on the sidewalks, flats of blooming pansies and garden-ready tomato plants invited us to take them home.

Here a store was advertising "Adirondack" chairs with plywood frames. And there a motel called itself "Alpine" and featured pseudo-European decor. Unperturbed by all these fashions, the gray rock faces of the patient mountains looked back to a time before these trends and forward beyond them.

The half-grown leaves of popple and birch trees fluttered like chartreuse suncatchers in the breeze, a contrast to the stately dark green spruce and balsam trees nearby.

And here the store front planters at the Summer Store were still waiting to be planted with flowers and the weathered plank benches by the sidewalk were still waiting to comfort tired tourists.

And there a small boat floated at dockside with four pairs of knees hanging over the side, baking in the sun. Villagers in shorts and tank tops went leisurely about their errands. A top-down convertible, rolled by with bearded, shirtless driver enjoying this early touch of summer.

Heels echoed on board steps—a sound that will be lost later amid the clomp and jostle of in-season crowds.

And timeless, here and there along the highway, were the huddled gray stick mounds of beaver lodges, and the simple white elegance of woodland trilliums, and water seeping out of rock ledges, and wayside streams splashing merrily over the stones.

I tell you all this because I know many of you cannot take the time just now to go and savor these things for yourself, and I wanted to share some of these country blessings with you.

Priceless

We own such lovely treasures—
    a warming springtime sun,
a roadside view of woodlands
    where saucy squirrels run,
a chance to smell the blossoms
    and hear the robins call,
but most of all, a thankful heart
    to share it with you all.

Education for Life

1993

"Why didn't they teach us that in school?" His pale blue eyes were filled with puzzlement. "They taught me a lot of things I haven't used since. But they never told me there was a difference between how males and females think!"

This friend of ours, now past 50, is still trying to figure out the female mind. Cautious and observant, he doesn't want to become emotionally involved until he's sure he has found the right woman. "Good Luck!", we tell him, but we're not at all sure he'll ever find what he's looking for. Another thing they didn't teach us in school is that there is no such thing as the ideal person.

A friend with young children discovered her husband was introducing their children to sex play. Appalled, she left him with the aid of another man. But school had not taught her that knights in shining armor may be deceptive. He was soon coming home drunk, beating her up, and kicking her children out of the house.

A young couple we know were married several years ago, before divorce was rampant. The custom then was for girls to marry young, raise a family, stay at home and make mothering their career. She did this faithfully. But the military took him away for long stretches. And when he came home, he wanted some excitement. His wife, busy with children, was not very exciting. Just loyal and hard working. He soon found excitement elsewhere. But he was devastated when his dalliance cost him his marriage. He still *loved* his wife! Why hadn't anyone warned him about such things?

A young mother of today is having problems with a rebellious teenager. The teen demands to know why the mother makes such unreasonable rules. The mother simply says, "I didn't have any training for parenthood. I'm learning on the job. From past experience I figure this is the best way to go, so that's what's going to happen. Period."

A sixteen-year-old dropped out of school. He had an undetected learning disability. A brilliant man, he still struggles with things that have to be read or written. But he can work circles around most of his contemporaries.

Another man was a genius in school, taking top honors in math and science classes. He was articulate and analytical. But he never learned to interact easily with other people. Except for a very small circle of acquaintances he is a loner.

I tell you all these things because I think there is a huge gap in our educational system, a lack of teaching human relations skills that is crippling millions. Years ago, when the church was the center of community life, circumstances like those recounted above were the exception rather than the rule as they seem to be today.

The reason, I believe, is that the church, by being the center of a community's social life as well as its spiritual life, became, in essence, one huge extended family. Children and struggling young parents had dozens of experienced role models in this extended family setting. If any stepped out of line, the whole community frowned and pointed them back to the straight and narrow.

When this happened, the individual experienced a vital progression rarely seen in our school-centered society. First, they were called to account, made aware that they were responsible for their own actions. They were told and shown what is the acceptable way to act. Next, they were given a chance to make restitution where possible. Finally, they were forgiven for their wrong behavior and restored to their former standing. They, and others, learned well from the experience and became even more valued members of the community.

As times changed, so did society. The churches established public schools for the education of their children. At first, the Bible was a major textbook in those schools. From it, children learned not only spiritual guidance but respect for elders, fair play, giving others a chance, and responsibility. They learned to appreciate different kinds of literature and philosophy, history and poetry, for they were all there.

Then the schools decided to ban the Bible from the curriculum. Gradually, anything pertaining to the church was frowned on and pushed aside. Prayer was outlawed. And the school, which had been established by the church, turned against its "parent" like a rebellious adolescent and cut all ties.

Instead of concentrating on the growth of character in children, the schools began instead to concentrate on the growth of physical skills, strength, competitiveness and endurance. The question of how to interact with others on a social and moral basis was lost in the rush for everyone to excel in physical fitness.

Teachers who recognize the value in non-athletic students, are to be commended. The philosopher, diplomat, parent and entrepreneur all need encouragement, too. We must teach them, not just how to make a living, but how to *live*.

Honoring Mentors

We honor the teachers, parents and friends
Who help us to be our best,
Whether in sports or study or play,
Or involved in a lifelong quest
To better the world in which we live,
Or discover a new frontier,
Or help a child who has lost its way,
Or establish a new career.
We thank all those who encourage us
Through all of our joys and fears,
Who laugh and cry and comfort and care
And cherish us through our years.

Patriot

1994

Here we are, sandwiched in between Memorial Day and Flag Day, feeling patriotic and proud of our heritage. Some of us have had a hand in shaping what our country is. Many of us enjoy the fruits of the labors of a few. Some of us have grumbled and complained the whole way, but we are celebrating anyway— remembering the "pilgrims' feet", the "heroes proved", and the "patriots' dream" as we sing about this land we call "America the Beautiful".

And yet, if we want those beautiful sentiments to be more than empty words, we have to wise up. We need to take a good look at this "land of the free and home of the brave" in which we live. Just as any home needs repairs and maintenance, so does this one. Just as we would check the stability of the foundations of the houses in which we live, making sure the mortar isn't crumbling, frost has not cracked the walls and radon isn't seeping in, so we need to check the foundations of the home we call America.

Ever since the foundation stones were laid, the mortar of hard work, honesty, integrity and fair play has kept our house strong. But now we see the disintegration of the work ethic. We see millions seeking a something-for-nothing life—easy money, handouts. Our overburdened welfare system, lotteries sanctioned by the government, numerous wealth-promising game shows on television—all shout that the "radon" of greed and indolence is seeping through our walls.

Almost weekly, we hear news about dishonesty in high places—questionable investments, misuse of public property at taxpayer expense, manipulation, gross disregard for the intent of our nation's founders, blank-check spending of the public's hard earned dollars. All these abuses and excesses should sound an urgent warning that our beautiful America is in grave danger of crumbling.

The old saying, "power corrupts", was never more true than it is right now. And yet, those who speak out against what is going on are ridiculed, discredited and defamed. That is nothing new. The religious establishment ridiculed John the Baptist as "a voice crying in the wilderness". Joseph Lister was ridiculed by the medical establishment for insisting that surgeons should wash their hands between autopsies and infant deliveries, to prevent the spread of disease. The Wright Brothers were ridiculed by the scientific establishment for daring to suggest that men could fly.

And today's hard working citizens are ridiculed and ignored by the political establishment when they say it is unconscionable and immoral for legislators—servants of the people—to determine their own pay scale and to live more luxuriously than millions of those whose sweat and toil underwrite this travesty.

From a practical standpoint we need a minimum of three things.

*We need initiative and referendum legislation. This would give citizens the right to propose legislation and it would give the voters the right to pass or reject it.

*We need a line-item veto to prevent passage of unwanted legislation by tacking unrelated amendments onto bills which are popular and will pass.

*We need an independent commission to establish and regularly re-evaluate the salaries and benefits of all elected officials—at all levels of government. Members of each commission should represent a true cross section of our society and should serve on a rotating basis so that no one becomes entrenched and corrupted by power.

From a spiritual standpoint, we desperately need a return to the principles on which our nation was founded. Our founders saw the evils of the Church ruling the Crown and of the Crown ruling the Church. To prevent such abuses in this country they gave us the first amendment to the Constitution:

"Congress shall make no law respecting an establishment of religion, or prohibiting the free exercise thereof; or abridging the freedom of speech, or of the press; or the right of the people peaceably to assemble, and to petition the Government for a redress of grievances."

Unfortunately, anti-religion/anti-Christian zealots have taken it upon themselves to do what Congress is prohibited from doing. They have prohibited the free exercise of religion by outlawing prayer in public schools. They have established instead a religion of sports in which the star athletes are the gods; the cheer leaders are the vestal virgins (or otherwise); the coaches are the priests and priestesses; interscholastic and intercollegiate competitions are the worship services; and students who do not participate, or are not interested, are looked upon as inferior or flawed.

Not only have we mislaid the spiritual principles which made our country viable, not only have we forgotten the foundations of education that made our leaders truly great, we have substituted the trivial, the unimportant, the immoral and the amoral.

Here we are, sandwiched between Memorial Day and Flag Day, feeling as if something is not quite right. And in truth, something is *not* right. We have lost our soul. We are floundering in the dark waters of a troubled ocean. Our masts are broken and our compass damaged and we have forgotten that the One who made us is waiting to help, only He will not force his help upon us.

"Blessed is the nation whose God is the *Lord*." In all our days of remembering, let us remember *that*.

The Patriot's Dream

"Oh, beautiful for spacious skies,"
Our voices sing. Our hopes are pinned
On lovely thoughts of "fruited plain".
While fruits of righteousness lie crushed
And we are led astray by lies.
We long to see again the wind
Caressing "amber waves of grain"
And stirring in our souls, long hushed.

"Oh, beautiful for pilgrims' feet,"
That walked this land from sea to sea,
Discovering gold not yet refined--
The gold of peace and liberty.
And having won that precious street,
They passed it on to you and me,
A model for all humankind,
A "home of the brave," a "land of the free."

"Oh, beautiful for heroes proved,"
Who fill our memories today,
Inspiring us to greater deeds,
To build a nation strong and sure,
A nation that cannot be moved
When Godless forces hold their sway,
But one that meets its people's needs
For truth and love. We *shall* endure!

"Oh, beautiful for patriot dream,"
That draws us on to do our best,
That helps us learn from lessons past
To banish prejudice and hate,
To look beyond things as they <u>seem</u>,
To put new theories to the test,
To choose the good that's bound to last.
Then shall this land be truly great!

Gardening

June 1995

"A cold, wet May--a barn full of hay." At least that's what the oldtimers used to tell us. Well, I have a little to add to that. A cold, wet June--they'll sing another tune. June, of course, is Dairy Month, and it's during this month that the greatest portion of the hay is harvested and stored away to feed those dairy cows during the long winter. A few farmers even started the process on some of those nice warm, sunny days we had in late May (oh, yes, there were a few).

Now it's time for the weather to settle down and do some summer for us. We'd all appreciate it after a late, snowy winter and a spring that was mainly gray and drenching. I like to think of it as liquid sunshine, with the warm, dry kind just around the corner. For if the oldtimers were right, another of their prognostications will kick in soon enough.

"If the oak leafs out before the ash, there'll be a summer of mud and splash," they said. Have you noticed how late the ash trees got their leaves this year in comparison to the oaks?

Enough about the weather. It's time to turn our thoughts to all those summer joys and summer jobs that lie just ahead. Is your garden planted yet? When we were on the farm, Memorial Day was the traditional time for planting garden.

I get tired now just thinking about the size of garden I used to manage each year. But it was healthy work, for me and for the children. Some years they had individual plots where they grew their own choice of vegetables and flowers. And if the weather was kind and the bugs stayed away, they'd have ribbon-winning produce to enter in 4-H competition at the Lewis County Fair.

That seems like a whole lifetime ago. And in a way, it is. We were different people then. Just as the vegetables grew and matured and were "graduated" from their sunny garden beds, so the children all grew and matured and were "graduated" into lives quite different from the row-on-row predictability of school life.

They ranged across the map from Albany to Houston, South Carolina, Washington State, California and Rhode Island. They plied trades from carpentry to nursing, vacuum cleaner sales to Tupperware management, woodcutting to childcare, housepainting to custom sewing, military service, building inspection, TV cable installation, store clerking, power dam repair, apartment complex management and heavy equipment operation. One even ended up being a farmer!

I tell you all this because I think gardens and families are very much alike. We prepare the soil and we prepare a stable home environment. We mark off rows in the garden where we plant the seeds and wait for them to push up through the warm soil and stretch up into the sunshine. We set up a crib and read how-to-be-a-good-parent books and wait. Will it be a boy or a girl?!

We rejoice when the first tender peas are ready to pick and when the first round, red radishes appear. And we rejoice when the new baby comes home and adds its voice to the family conversations.

We cultivate the garden rows to give roots room to expand, and we pull weeds to keep them from choking the young vegetables. We teach our children how to brush their teeth and make their beds and we monitor their TV watching to keep the weeds of bad ideas from choking their young minds.

When the ground is dry, we refresh our growing vegetables and flowers with water, and maybe some added fertilizer. When our children's lives are dry from discouragement or difficulty, we refresh them with hugs and encouragement, and maybe a special treat or surprise.

When the vegetables are just right, we harvest them and turn them into delicious meals. We pick the flowers and make lovely bouquets to share with others. When the children are just right, or as near as we can bring them to it, we send them off to college or to work or to a home of their own where they add zest and value to the community around them, and where they produce lovely "bouquets" of grandchildren to share with us.

Far fetched? Not if we use a little imagination. And that's what makes it fun to come this far and pause to look back at all the "gardens" we have planted.

Garden Variety

Gardens of vegetables, gardens of flowers,
Gardens of singing and story-filled hours,
Gardens where learning and growing and giving
Strengthen the young "plants" for vigorous living.
Gardens for work and gardens for play--
Hoeing and weeding and laughing away.
Gardens of sunshine and wind in the hair,
Growing tho weather be fearsome or fair.
Planting for safety in row upon row,
Harvesting gladly when time comes to go.
Working so patiently, year after year,
Joyful when fullness of fruit shall appear.
Doing our best, and resting. And then--
Giving the world new women and men!

Never too old to Learn

1993

We went to Frankfort on Thursday, where 55-Alive instructors from all over the area met for their annual workshop. For those who aren't familiar with 55-Alive, it is a popular classroom course in defensive driving for motorists age 50 and over.

I know some of you will say, "What do senior citizens need with a classroom course in driving? They've been at it for years!" That, of course, is just the point. Things have changed over those years. Highways have changed, many from narrow two-lane roads to sleek ribbons of adventure four, six, even eight lanes wide.

Cars have changed, too. The boxy, dependable old Model T has been replaced by the sophisticated, high-powered Lincoln. And with these smoother, wider roads and more powerful cars, have come much higher speed limits than those in effect when many oldsters learned to drive. Super highways require different driving techniques than those we used on country lanes.

Even the New York State Driver's Manual has changed. As recently as 1958, the manual was pocket size, about three by five inches with 48 pages of text and illustrations. Today's manual is a bulkier five by seven inches with twice as many pages of instructions, illustrations and regulations. Of course we need refreshers! If you're past 50, how much do you remember of what you learned in highschool Latin or geometry or chemistry? It's the same with driving.

Don has been teaching 55-Alive for probably six or seven years and it's not true that "you can't teach an old dog new tricks." Most students who take the defensive driving classes say they either learned something new, or were reminded of something they once knew but had forgotten. Not only that, but seasoned older drivers often have had experiences which taught them valuable safety lessons which they share with other class members.

These are the kinds of things 55-Alive instructors share when they get together for their annual in-service training. They hear from motor vehicle department representatives who let them know about new changes coming. They hear from other senior volunteers about how well we're implementing this helpful, cost-saving service.

Did you know that New York State ranked first for number of students completing 55-Alive in 1992! Instructors were taking a pleasant pat on the back for that fact when another statistic tumbled out on top of it: Only 2% of eligible New York State drivers bothered to take advantage of the program last year!

The group began brainstorming about reasons for the lack of participation. One said many folks probably don't realize the insurance premium savings they get by taking the course. Another commented that some are afraid they'll have to cope with a written exam in order to pass. Not so. It was also suggested that many older folks might be afraid they'd be required to take another road test. Also not so.

In this area, Lewis County Cooperative Extension has been a great help in hosting the classes each month, publicizing course dates, and including other pertinent information of interest to prospective students. This is not only a valuable public service, it also makes our streets and roads safer for all drivers. That little old lady with gray hair tooling by in her fancy red van may be one of the safest drivers you'll meet--once she has taken the course.

This area is fortunate to have several instructors available. And what do these dedicated folks earn for their efforts? Few people realize they are all volunteers! They are paid mileage and expenses only. The small fee charged to students covers the cost of materials and of registering with the motor vehicle department the names of those who have completed the course. Even the area and state coordinators volunteer their time.

Money isn't everything, though. Making new friends, doing something useful for the community, developing new skills, enjoying the interchange of ideas and experiences—all these are the dividends that keep instructors dedicated to their jobs. They make 55-Alive one of the most successful and fastest growing "shoestring" programs in the country.

I tell you all this because I think it is just another example of how life is enriched for all of us when people go out of their way to help other people without grasping for rewards. Our society has put too much emphasis on money.

I learned more from my parents and Sunday School teachers—volunteers, all—than from the people who were paid to teach me in school. More about how to live. More about how to relate to other people. More about how to think and reason. More about compassion and forgiveness. More about privilege and responsibility. More about fantasy. More about freedom. More about fun.

And those folks didn't wait until they were retired to give of their time, either. It was part of the culture in which I grew up—neighbor helping neighbor for the good of all.

Old Fashioned Ideas

Now money is nice if you need to buy rice
Or potatoes or hot dogs or cheese.
It comes in right handy when purchasing candy
Or sneakers or toothpaste or peas.
But money, or none, you can always have fun
By sharing a laugh with a friend,
By picnicking, playing, gardening, praying,
Without being "broke" in the end.
And stories go well and are easy to tell,
And all they will cost is your time.
And a fun afternoon, singing tune after tune,
Won't cost you so much as a dime.

When problems assail, don't sit there and wail
About what a mess life has made.
With work and a song you can solve it e'er long
If you don't always have to be paid.
Tho cash is a must if it's "Paris or Bust!"
You can always find alternate pleasure
By lending a hand. In fact, you'll feel grand!
Where your heart is—that's really the treasure.

Disappointments

1995

When I was three, there wasn't much of anything I liked better than riding in a car. For us, it was a once-a-year treat, enjoyed when Aunt Bessie and Uncle Will made the annual trip from their home in Seneca Falls to Oswegatchie, where we lived.

I remember Uncle Will used to tease us by calling our baby brother "Jim-Lahrie", when his real name was Larry Jim. And Aunt Bessie, whenever she exclaimed about something, would say, "My stars and garters!" Aunt Bessie fussed over me and made me feel special because she had no children of her own. Naturally I adored her and decided, that when I grew up, I'd have bedroom wallpaper with stars and garters on it in honor of Aunt Bessie.

When I was three, Aunt Bessie brought some dress material, a tiny rosebud print, for Mother to make me a dress. There was enough to make matching panties and bonnet, which really made me feel dressed up. I remember wearing the outfit to church. During prayer, Mother had taught me to bow my head. And I thought how nice it was that church made a special time for people to sit and look at their new dresses and enjoy them.

Later that summer I was playing with my friend Inez when her mother said I'd have to go home because they were getting ready to go to town. As I said, I had a real passion for riding in a car, so I asked if I could go with them. Her mother said she couldn't take me unless my mother said so.

Excitedly, I hurried across the street to our house, but my mother wasn't there. She was out back in the garden. I needed to go to the toilet, but asking mother was more urgent. I ran to where she was kneeling and stumbled over my words telling her about my ride. She said she'd have to know where they were going before she'd say yes. So I rushed back to Inez' house, ignoring my other urgency, and found they'd left already. The let down was total. I went crying back to Mother, who left her work and went to get dry clothes for me.

When I was four, Aunt Bessie asked permission to take me home with her for a week. Now *that* was a *ride*! Mother said I could go, and you can believe I was excited. All my other rides had been comparatively short ones, to the doctor at Newton Falls, the Sunday school picnic at Cranberry Lake, and pleasant little rides with Uncle Will.

We traveled what seemed like forever. I was actually tired of riding before Uncle Will finally said, "Here we are." I looked, but couldn't see any house, just big tall buildings. We had to walk up a long flight of stairs to get to their apartment. That certainly was strange. I was used to going up stairs only when it was bedtime. But by this time it nearly was. We ate, and Aunt Bessie got me ready for bed. There was a lamp with a pretty pink shade on it by my bedside.

The next day, Aunt Bessie went about her housework as usual, almost forgetting I was there. I climbed up on the tall stool in her little kitchen so I could watch her better and she said, "Oh, you can't sit there. That's where the iceman sets his block of ice while he's opening the icebox to put it in. It's almost time for him to come." I'd never seen an iceman, but already I didn't like him. There was no place for me. I began to miss my mother's big kitchen and the way she talked with me while she worked and even let me help her.

At bedtime, Aunt Bessie got into her nightgown and put on a puffy nightcap. I'd never seen anybody wear a nightcap before. She didn't look like Aunt Bessie with that strange thing on her head. I wanted to go home. She said it was too late at night to go, we'd wait and see how I felt in the morning. That night I dreamed Aunt Bessie was a bear, and I woke up crying. In the morning we loaded the car and headed for Oswegatchie again.

When I was turning five, Aunt Bessie wrote and asked mother what I wanted for my birthday. I had just been to a birthday party for Beverly. Her mother had given her a beautiful pair of pink patent leather shoes with thin buckle straps. *That's* what I wanted. I knew this would be a good birthday. But it came and went without a package arriving from Aunt Bessie. A letter came explaining that she hadn't been able to find pink shoes yet, but had a couple of other stores to check.

When the package finally came, I couldn't wait to open it and get my beautiful new pink shoes. Instead, there was a pair of pink fuzzy slippers. She hadn't been able to find pink shoes, and hoped these would satisfy. They were too small, and went to my little sister instead.

I tell you all these things because disappointments are such a common denominator among human beings. Everyone experiences them. It's how we react to them that determines our outlook on life. Little children have to learn this the hard way.

Mother helped to ease my hurt feelings by cuddling me, helping me to find the good in each situation, and telling me stories about children who had their own way all the time and ended up not being very likeable.

Pollyanna, that fictional childhood heroine who always found something good in every person and in every situation, had more going for her than we suppose. Some call her an impossible, unrealistic idealist. I say, "Hooray! Good for her." We never achieve high if we aim low. And happiness only comes to us when we are in a frame of mind to recognize it and appreciate it.

Dealing with Disappointments

Disappointments and hurt feelings
are a lot like caterpillars—
They crawl
and chew our leaves—
those peace-of-mind leaves
that deck our tree of life.

A little spray of common sense
can help to stop those worms
and keep our peace intact.
A mist of other interests
can wash away the dust and droppings
and freshen up our days.

Disappointments,
like dark clouds,
give way before the winds of fresh ideas
and the warm sunshine
of honest gratitude.

Poets' Picnic

1995

On the first day of summer I spent a delightful afternoon in a candlelit cafe, sipping herb lemonade and visiting with friends both new and old. Advance notices had heralded the event as "The Poets' Picnic", a gathering "for those who think they don't like poetry, for those who forgot they did, and for those who find joy in creativity, or need to."

We who accepted the invitation found ourselves in a carefully arranged ambience, set in the cool basement of the library. Here we were shielded from the heat of the year's most direct sun rays, where no sudden gusts of wind riffled our picnic plates. The mood was undisturbed by busy traffic noises and only a pleasant, congenial setting prevailed, where we savored both food for the body and food for the spirit.

In one corner, Patricia sat on a high stool, strummed her guitar softly and sang to us about an old river calling us back, back from the busy city ways, back from the bustle of things to do, back to the peacefulness of home and loved ones.

Then she shared with us poems about nature and its bounty, special animals and very special people in her life. As she read, she accompanied her word images with colored slides, drawing us in to her experiences and feelings. She ended with a hilarious song about the ark, seen through the eyes of Mrs. Noah, bearing discomforts bravely since it was, after all, the only ship afloat.

Other poets were then invited to read from their works and some did. I am always amazed at the depth and variety in such a presentation. Poetry topics ranged from an old house with a picket fence and swinging gate, to a jarring news photo of Bosnian casualties, from a bit of life philosophy to a bumpy dump truck ride, from autumn harvest bounty to a piece of forgotten tinsel.

I am convinced there is poetry in each of us. It takes as many different forms as there are people willing to express it. Some of the slides Patricia showed were poetic images themselves, touching our senses and imaginations, moving us to laughter or tears, leading us into contemplation.

Some individuals have this gift, this ability to put visual images together in a way that evokes memories and emotions. Others do it with music and still others with words. A few express their poetic nature in motion—dance, gymnastics, choreography. Others spread colors on canvas and draw us into their moods and rhythms through painting. All these expressions are forms of poetry.

Occasionally I read good prose that is rich in poetic feeling. It doesn't rhyme, of course. It doesn't have to. But it does capture the reader's attention and tickle the mind with its delectable choice of words. Good poetry often does that.

In a way, all poetry is good. By that I do not mean it is pleasing to all hearers or readers. Much of what passes for poetry is not pleasing at all. But it serves as a vehicle for the sharing of thoughts and feelings, impressions, despairs and hopes. It is good because it helps us dig out and look at issues, long buried, that may still affect us. It is good because it helps us deal with present hurts, doubts and adversities in ways that promote healing. I call it therapeutic verse.

The urge to give expression to deep feelings is universal. It is one reason I say there is poetry in each of us. Poetry flows from us, spoken or not. Sometimes it is simply for our own enjoyment. Sometimes it helps us process pain. Some poetry is private; some can be shared. We may not see ourselves as poetic but there is a rhythm and a beauty in our lives that denies our negative statements to the contrary.

I would like to see more gatherings of poets, of creative thinkers, of individuals who thrill at earth's beauty and ponder life's deep questions. Our busy technological society has squeezed poetry to the fringes of life and denied its importance. But it cannot silence that life spark that gives poets a sense of the mysterious, the precious, the awesome, the serene expanses within and around us.

Celebrate Life

Celebrate life in all its complexity—
flowing through joy,
perplexity, pain,
questions and doubts,
triumphs and sadness,
unspoken gladness,
unresolved shame.

These are the stones that build our humanity.
These give us substance
and meaning
and grace—
chiseling, carving,
cutting and sanding—
shaping the character lines on each face.

Out of the depths of all our experience,
out of the heights of sought-after goals,
God,
the Great Poet,
sifts out the essence,
healing
and filling
and blessing our souls.

Square

1995

The story is told of a man who was looking for someone to build a house for him. Now a certain carpenter who had some experience lived nearby. Anxious to improve his expertise, his reputation and his income, he asked for the job. He had never managed a project like this before, but was confident he could do it successfully.

The two men sat down together and discussed dimensions, types of materials to be used, placement of doors and windows, and all the dozens of other details necessary for such an undertaking. The carpenter made a careful list of needed materials and priced them out at nearby suppliers. Then he gave the prospective homeowner an estimate, including the cost of his labor, and the two shook hands on the deal. Materials were ordered and the work commenced.

The framing was all up and the sheathing was going on when a neighbor noticed things didn't look right. The homeowner and his neighbor measured the building and found it wasn't square at the corners. In fact, one wall was several inches shorter than the one opposite. The carpenter made excuses about the foundation not being set just right. But he was sure everything would smooth out and look fine when he finished.

Too much time and money for materials had already been spent, so the homeowner made do with what was there, rather than investing more time and money, and rather than penalizing the poor carpenter who really needed the work. The carpenter, of course, felt bad.

Rather than improving his expertise and boosting his ego, the job had turned into a nightmare of small mistakes which he tried to work around, but which made his work twice as hard and only half as satisfactory as it would have been if done right in the first place.

I tell you this story because building a house is a lot like building a reputation, a friendship, a career or a marriage. If the house is to be square, the reputation honorable, the friendship true, the career successful, the marriage enduring—if all these are to stand the test of time, we must prepare carefully. No matter how good our intentions, we must lay a square, solid foundation.

There are many quirks in our society. One is that people think their house corners should be square, but their friends shouldn't be. That idea would be amusing if it were not so sad. For some reason, many people would rather die than be considered "square".

To me, a person who is square is honest, trustworthy, dependable, intelligent (even if not highly educated), kind, thoughtful of others, not given to bragging or boisterousness or foul language. A person who is square will give an honest day's work for an honest day's pay and will not seek to cut corners nor defraud the employer. A person who is square will not manipulate others for personal advantage, but will cheerfully lend a helping hand to make life better. A person who is square does not expect something for nothing, but tries to carry a fair share of the load.

Now that sounds to me like the kind of person I'd like to have for a friend. It also sounds like the kind of friend I want to be. The only reason I can think of for anyone to belittle someone for being "square", is found in this old proverb: "A man that has no virtue in himself envies it in others." Envy leads to putdowns.

Aesop immortalized this human foible in a fable. Remember how the fox saw some beautiful ripe grapes hanging from a trellis, but couldn't reach them? After trying everything to get at that tempting feast, but all in vain, the fox declared she didn't want the grapes anyway because they were undoubtedly sour.

If we are wise, we will take time to stop and rethink what we are about and where we want to be headed. The "popular" way is not always the best way to look at things, nor to achieve a purpose.

For many of us, personally and socially, educationally and economically, this is a period of rapid change. Without laying a square foundation for the coming years, we put ourselves in danger of building a weak structure for our lives. When you think of it that way, square isn't such a bad idea after all.

Building for Life

The carpenter planned his work for the day with care.
He laid out hammer and saw, stout nails, and a square.
He measured and cut and fitted and hammered until
The house he was building stood firm and square on its hill.

A young lass looked at the years that stretched ahead.
I'd like to be a special ed teacher, she said.
So she helped with a neighbor's multiply-handicapped son.
She studied and worked until her diploma was won.
Then, using the firm foundation of knowledge she'd learned,
She lightened the load for those whose affection she earned.

"I love you," each said. "Let us spend our lifetime as one."
So they laid a foundation of faithfulness, honor and home,
Respecting each other, learning and growing each year,
Sharing and caring, holding each other dear.

The house, career and marriage all eased life's care,
And each endured its trials, for each was SQUARE.

Family Values

2001

"We stand for family values."

Everyone says that. It was a major catchphrase around the turn of the new millennium, especially during the political campaigns. But we often notice that those who use the phrase couldn't be farther apart in their meaning. We wonder--what does the phrase "family values" really mean?

I think of the sun, shining brightly, just as that phrase does. And I think of the pictures of the sun my children drew, with its rays spreading out in all directions. Those rays serve different purposes—some give light; some give heat; some create plant growth through photosynthesis; some affect people's psychological moods; some dance through prisms and turn into beautiful rainbows; some melt the snow, draw crocuses up out of the ground and send birds winging northward.

The shining phrase "family values" sends out rays in all directions, too—rays of interpretation. Some interpret family values to mean having a dependable day care so both parents can work and bring home money enough to afford the life style to which they have become accustomed.

Some think of family values as discount sales where children's clothing and other necessities can be purchased at reduced prices.

Some picture Mother staying at home with the children, instilling discipline, courtesy, helpfulness and obedience while Father earns a living for them all.

Some see family values as allowing homosexual lovers to marry and raise children just like anyone else.

Some envision State-run daycare centers for all children, leaving parents free to pursue fulfilling careers, and making sure uniform training occurs for children so that everyone grows up to be politically correct in their thinking.

Some see family values as an excuse to give in to the boyfriend once again because another baby means a bigger welfare check, and more money equals nicer things.

Family values can mean making God the head of your household and trying to raise your children and do your work in ways that will honor that commitment. Or it can mean making money the head of your household and spending all energies in that direction. It can mean playing together, praying together, exercising together, or working together in a family-run business.

When I was a small child, my parents took us for nature walks. We picked roadside flowers, netted and identified various butterflies, became familiar with different kinds of trees and birds. We played games together, sang songs together, went to church together, prayed bedtime prayers together, ate meals together and listened to stories together.

My package of family values began to take shape, even without my being aware of them. And togetherness was one of the major ingredients.

Each of us is shaped, and our ideas of family values are shaped, by our early childhood experiences. But the process doesn't end there. It is a growing and continuing process and lasts a lifetime. Usually we don't even stop to think about what is happening, but it happens anyway. I found it brings life into sharper focus, this taking time to analyze my family values and how they grew.

When I was five, my parents were divorced—the family togetherness shattered. But I clung to that value. It was part of my very core of being. I *knew* I would never divorce and put my children through the kind of tornness and alienation I had felt.

All the time I was growing up, church attendance was a given. There was no question that church was part of the bedrock on which my life and perceptions developed. In times of crisis I really needed that support network, that stability. And when I was alone, crying into my pillow, I needed that sure knowledge that God was there and was in control, and that eventually he would bring me through the trials. That deep-rooted certainty became an integral part of my family value system.

I was raised during the Great Depression. Money was scarce and luxuries were rare. I learned very early to appreciate and care for whatever I had. I never took for granted even the smallest blessings—until I grew up and everything changed. *Things* became plentiful. The society around me developed a mindset that seemed to say, "The world owes us a living." I fell into the trap of taking my good fortune for granted. When a major economic depression in farming hit, in the early 1980s, it jarred me back to reality, but not before I went through a serious depression myself.

Sometimes I have to be reminded of the things I already know. Family and friends helped to remind me, during my depression, of the things that really mattered in life—physical health, a grateful heart, loving family. Often we'd drive up on the hill and look out across the peaceful valleys of this beautiful land and it would calm my troubled mind and give me a different perspective on problems that had seemed insurmountable.

I tell you all these things because I suspect I'm not the only person who goes through troubling experiences and needs a change in perspective once in a while. If I can help anyone by sharing what I've been through, it will be worth it.

Someone once asked me why I smile so much and I replied that smiling is easier than frowning or crying. I should know—I've done my share of those, too. And smiling *is* easier. Every situation in our lives has many sides. We can choose to look at the gloomy side, the hopeless side, the cheerful side, the opportunities, the long-range benefits and possibilities or the neutral, detached sides of the issue. Whatever way we wish to see it, the choice *is* ours.

And so I have added to my family values system the exercise of a cheerful outlook. I have learned along the way to be kind to myself and to others. I have learned to look for the positive side of whatever comes into my life. And I have tried to share these values with my family and friends.

Whenever

Whenever the snow is much too deep,
Or the summer sun too hot,
Whenever the bills are much too big,
And the weekly check is not,
Whenever the supper is burned again,
Or the waitress seems too slow,
When the old cat misses the litter box
Or your shoe is pinching your toe,
Whenever the mailman doesn't stop
With the letter you hoped would come,
Whenever you find yourself stuck fast
In a misplaced wad of gum,
Remember, it's better by far to smile,
Than to grumble or cuss or frown.
Be thankful. Be cheerful. Be gentle.
Then troubles can *not* get you down.

Birds and other blessings

1997

I woke before six. The lengthening days of spring have that effect on me. It makes a good opportunity to do some of the quiet tasks of the day before the rest of the household begins to stir. Outside the window, I can hardly see the sky, the leaves are so thick on the big maple trees. They have grown so fast I am sometimes surprised to realize it isn't winter any more.

Somewhere nearby a pair of brilliant orioles is nesting. We saw one here once before, on its way somewhere else. But this year both the male and female have stayed around, drinking the sugar water from the hummingbird feeders through their long, slender beaks. We have one of Adam Seletyn's weather sticks mounted outside the dinette window where we can keep track of the humidity level, informally. The male oriole sat on that stick the other day and chirped at his reflection in the window glass, even pecked at it several times, protecting his territory.

All winter long we kept seed in the bird feeders in the back yard. Other years have seen a profusion of evening grosbeaks, blue jays, mourning doves, nuthatches, chickadees, house finches and sparrows coming there to eat. But this past winter, we had hardly any visitors at all. Not even the usual squirrels.

But this spring is a different story. Our yard has been alive with birds most of the time. Gold finches have adorned the crabapple-like ornaments on a Christmas tree. They fill the six perches on the hanging feeder and take turns shuttling back and forth to the nearby branches.

And in among them, we caught a glimpse of a most unusual sight—indigo buntings! We saw a single migrating indigo several years ago, but there were three at once here one day this spring. And there is still one I see occasionally, a real treat.

Another rarity at this particular spot is the rose breasted grosbeak. But we have seen one pair several times recently. They must be nesting nearby. Surprisingly absent all winter, the downy woodpecker now comes to peck at the chunk of suet hung in the apple tree. The mourning doves are back, picking up spills of seed underneath the hanging feeder, along with purple grackles, cowbirds and sparrows.

The blue jay, absent most of the winter, is mixing his raucous call with that of his cousin the crow. And during quieter parts of the day, the robin tilts his head, listening for earthworms to give away their hiding place. Quiet, quick, and unruffled by all this activity, the tiny hummingbirds come to drink from the feeder right in front of the window. What a pleasure to watch!

Mo is fascinated by the goings-on outside her window. We jokingly call it the cat's big-screen TV. Her presence may startle the birds momentarily, but they come right back. They seem to realize she can't touch them from where she sits on the windowsill. Mo is short for Mozart, a name she acquired because she makes such beautiful music when she purrs. Mozart is white, with exceedingly long hair, and she is deaf. She lives inside because she could be run over by a car and never hear it coming.

Max, on the other hand, spends most of her summer outdoors or in the garage. Max, too, is white. But. Max loves to roll in the driveway and rub her back against the underside of parked vehicles. She never *looks* white. She too is fascinated by the birds, but rarely disturbs them. She caught one or two in her younger years and was roundly scolded for it. She probably figures it isn't worth it if we're not going to praise her efforts.

And now we have Tanner, an almost golden retriever looking lab mix who is four months old. He was smaller than the cats when we first brought him home, could almost walk underneath them. But he is fast overcoming that difficulty. He and Mo romp together like litter mates. She stirs things up to get him going, then tells him to back off when she's had enough.

Why am I telling you all these things? I think it's just a way of sharing my ambivalent feelings about pets. I never really wanted cats or dogs in the house; they shed so much hair and track in so much dirt. But I happen to have a husband who loves animals. What can I say? Pets are part of the territory. And so I adapt. After all, my pet lover helps by running the vacuum cleaner, buying the dog and cat food, filling the bird feeders and grooming the pets.

And on days when I feel pressured by deadlines or tired from other household tasks, the animal population brings a welcome distraction. I sit and watch the birds fill the yard with color and song. I take the pup for a walk. I stop to enjoy the sweet fragrance of crab apple blossoms and fresh mown lawn. I marvel at the intricate patterns of sunlight through leaves. And I know we are blessed.

Nature's Remedies

Life's little irritations, if we let them,
Will eat us up with worry and despair.
How fortunate we are to have distractions
That bless our souls with beauty everywhere.

The fragrance of the sweet crabapple blossoms,
The splash of brooks that laugh along their way,
The miracle of hummingbirds and hawthorns,
The joy of dogs and children at their play.

Life's little irritations lose their power
Beneath a gardener's turning of the sod,
And warming sun, with whisper-gentle breezes,
Lifts up the soul in thankfulness to God.

Audubon

1995

A bit of "trivia" caught my eye yesterday: On May 17, 1826, John J. Audubon left this country, "with deep sorrow", because he could not find a publisher for his bird pictures.

Now, I've noticed that what is commonly called trivia, is not actually trivial at all. In fact, there is often a fascinating story behind it. I tucked this bit of information in my possibility file and went looking for the story. Here is what I found.

Born in what is now Haiti, Audubon was the son of a Royal French Navy Lieutenant and his Creole mistress. When he was nine years old, Jean Jacques' father took him home to Nantes, France and presented him to his childless wife. She gladly adopted and raised the lad as her own.

Jean Jacques, who later adopted the Americanized version of his name, John James, had only one passion in life. He loved to draw pictures of birds. His keen observations and faithful reproduction of these fascinating creatures gave his life color and meaning. Altho his father sent him to study with a neo-classical artist, he did not stay long, preferring to teach himself through practice on his preferred subjects, the birds.

When John turned 18, his father sent him to America as business manager for Mill Grove, his estate in southeastern Pennsylvania, where he owned a lead mine. It was here that John tied silver threads around the legs of young phoebes in an effort to track their migrations. He is credited with being the first person in America to try gathering information by bird banding. He also met his future wife, Lucy Bakewell.

After they were married in 1808, they moved to Louisville and set up a general store. Lucy soon became involved in the busyness of raising a family. John's partner was more of a bookkeeper than a salesman, and John himself was often in the woods looking for more specimens of birds to paint. Needless to say, the store didn't do very well. They tried moving down river to a different location, but that didn't improve matters.

John J. Audubon suffered a series of financial reverses and finally ended up in debtors prison in 1819. The sheriff seized all his belongings to satisfy his debts. All except his portfolio of bird paintings, which the sheriff considered worthless.

When he was released, Audubon had nothing left to work with but he still had to earn a living. He went to work as a sidewalk artist, selling crayon portraits. He was so successful that he decided to move on to other regions. By this time, Lucy had taken work as a school teacher in Cincinnati.

Leaving the family behind, John took off on a bird painting adventure down the Ohio River in a flatboat. He took with him a thirteen-year-old boy named Joseph Mason, who was an artist in his own right. Mason added floral decorations to most of Audubon's bird paintings, making them look more natural and appealing. During this time Audubon also began keeping a diary of his adventures among the birds of his beloved adopted country.

In January, 1821, he reached New Orleans, penniless. But he made friends readily and always impressed them with his quick artistic ability. Very soon he had found a patron, a wealthy lady who hired him to tutor her daughter. He stayed in this position for five months, working in his off-duty hours on his own painting projects.

Within months his family was able to rejoin him. But again he began to suffer financial problems. And again the family moved, this time to Natchez. Here he taught French and drawing and even dancing, becoming very popular. Lucy found work, too, as governess on a plantation, again living apart from her husband. John continued with his portrait painting to earn a living. He also did decorative painting on the paneled walls of elegant river boats and even descended to painting street signs when business faltered.

All this time Audubon searched in vain for an American publisher for his paintings. Finally, a friend of his, a nephew of Napoleon Bonaparte, suggested he might better take his project to Europe, and pre-sell the books by subscription, a common practice in those days.

And so it was, that on May 17, 1826, John James Audubon left this land of opportunity, "with deep sorrow", to seek his opportunity in England. But his passion went with him. He spent much of the voyage sketching the ocean birds that circled his ship.

The following year, the first book of his four-volume set, "Birds of America", was completed. It was a monumental task, as each picture had to be translated to copper engraving plates which were used to print the pictures, then the illustrations were all hand colored. The work was such a success that he became a celebrity in England and much of Europe.

Not one to be idle, Audubon had also begun work on a five-volume set entitled "Ornithological Biography", a text intended as a companion set for the illustrated books already in production. By 1839, both sets had been completed and Audubon had been recognized at last, by his American compatriots, as an accomplished artist and naturalist.

His passion for painting was a driving force even after his spectacular success in Europe. He returned to America and pursued his beloved subjects through the Florida keys, into lagoons and along the sand dunes of the Texas coastline, northwest on the Missouri River, into North Dakota, and even among the thousand rocky islands of the St. Lawrence River. All this time he was documenting and sketching and beginning a new work entitled, "The Viviparous Quadrupeds of North America."

Unfortunately, ill health overtook him and he never finished all the projects he wanted to before his death in 1851. But the ones he did finish have become a monument to his powers of observation, his passion, and his persistence. The National Audubon Society, was formed to honor his genius. It is a living tribute to the man whose energy sparked a widespread appreciation for nature's variety and beauty.

Now you know why I say trivia is not necessarily trivial.

AUDUBON

A seed of genius sprouted and grew within his soul.
It spread thru nerve and muscle;it pushed him toward a goal.
Thru childhood paths it drew him,
    and down his grownup years
It nudged and urged and pummeled,
    tho washed by debtor's tears.

Relentlessly it hounded. Compelled to follow thru,
He pressed along new pathways. His genius thrived and grew.
His mind took wing; it lifted to soar thru bird-filled sky.
And then, with fingers gifted, translated wing and eye—

    A breathlessness of beauty,
        A glide of easy grace,
            A quiet, secret, hidden nest,
                A brooding feathered face.
    And year by year he traveled,
        And year by year he drew,
            Transforming nature's loveliness
                Thru all the paths he knew.

Cheat

1996

I heard a distressing story today. It concerns a high school where students figured out that a particular teacher gave the same tests each year. It was a simple matter to get copies of old tests and memorize the correct multiple-choice answers. Most of the students had excellent scores on tests all year and the teacher bragged about what good students they were. Several became members of the National Honor Society.

When the teacher handed out the final exam recently, one student refused to take it. When asked why, the student responded simply, "I'm the only one in this class who doesn't already have the answers."

The teacher, after hearing the details, rewrote the test, putting the questions in a different order. The average score of the students taking that teacher's tests had been in the high 90's all year. On the revised test, the average score was in the mid 40's. When the teacher confronted the class about the obvious cheating that had been going on, only four had the strength of character to admit their guilt.

Those four, and only those four, are being penalized. What a mixed message that is! In effect, the school authorities are saying it is dishonest to cheat and dishonesty is bad. But only those students who are dishonest enough to cover up, will get away with it. The ones honest enough to confess will be punished.

Compared to the others, who had respect for neither the teacher nor themselves, the four who confessed should be commended for their honesty. The test itself should point a convincing finger at all the other culprits. But, so far, the school authorities have chosen to look the other way.

I cannot verify this story from personal knowledge, but it came to me from a source I consider reliable. And just because it didn't happen to be "our" school, is no reason to ignore the implications. We can all learn something from such accounts if we pay attention.

As I said, I found the story distressing. When I began analyzing why, these were some of the reasons.

A teacher, who is supposed to be an educational resource and a model for the students, was made to look like a fool after praising their good marks all year. The teacher could have avoided this with a little extra effort expended in writing different tests instead of choosing the easy way.

When the students figured out what was going on, and actually followed the teacher's example by choosing the easy way, they were not cheating the teacher, but themselves. School is supposed to help prepare young people for life in the real world. It takes character to be able to struggle with life's tough questions, to make sound decisions, to develop innovative solutions for complex problems, to cope with the pressures and stresses of modern existence and to find satisfaction in what we do. The "easy way" never yet built that kind of character.

When an incident like this comes to light, it is human nature to try to lay blame at someone's door. We blame the kids for being dishonest. We blame the teacher for being lax and careless. We blame the parents for being too busy with their own concerns to notice what's happening in their children's lives. We blame the state for its school centralization plan where youngsters are reduced to numbers and no one notices when someone falls through the cracks in the system and kids act up to get attention.

But there is a proverb that couldn't be truer: "When you point a finger at someone else, there are three pointing back at you." Psychologists call it projection. We project our faults onto someone else so we don't have to face them in ourselves. We all do it.

My first reaction when I heard the story was to try to figure out how this could happen. Who was really to blame? But as I sit here thinking about it, I have to admit I often take the easy way out myself. I'm sometimes careless about details because I'd rather be doing something else. I hate to be caught not looking smart enough when it comes to the little "tests" that worm their way into my life frequently. And I expect most folks, if they were brutally honest with themselves, would admit the same.

The question, then, is not, "Who is to blame when kids cheat in school?" The question is, "How do I deal with these issues in my own life so that I can be a better role model for the children I know?" That's one that will keep me thinking for a while. I hope it will give each of you something to think about, too.

Kids don't need blame or punishment, scolding or grounding, fault finding or penalties nearly as much as they need honesty in the adults who are preparing them for life. Double standards don't work. Telling kids to, "do as I say, not as I do," is a cop-out.

Another thing kids really need is unconditional love from their families. So many children are disowned when they get caught doing something they shouldn't do. And that's another mixed message; it says, "I'll love you, but only if you don't embarrass or disgrace me." Yet how often those same parents say and do things to embarrass and humiliate the children.

People growing up in a difficult world need affirmation. When they do what is expected of them, what is right, they should be told their efforts are appreciated. If they make mistakes, someone needs to explain to them how it should be done. Patient instruction and encouragement have a much more positive effect on a young person's behavior and attitude than all the fault finding in the world.

Good role models are more important in life training than any other educational tool. Kids can sense "phony" a mile away. They're not stupid! They can read double standards and mixed messages better than they can read books. It doesn't do much for character to educate minds and exercise bodies if we neglect or deny emotional and spiritual needs.

Once again it is commencement time for graduating classes. Commencement marks the end of a particular phase of education. But it really means beginning, the beginning of the rest of life.

Thoughts on Life

So live,
That when the morning comes
And once again
Life beckons you
To follow untried paths,
You go not, as one
Disgraced by cheating,
But, stepping forth
With steady purpose
Born of careful preparation,
Approach each task with
Confidence, fearing not the
Barbs of envy, sprung from
Smallness and self-seeking.
But strive, instead, to
Champion the helpless,
Lift the fallen,
Encourage fellow travelers
And seek,
With courage and persistence,
The way of Truth and Right.

Flamingo

1998

I had almost forgotten about the flamingo babies. Then suddenly I rediscovered them. Five of them. Their furry lavender bodies huddled in a circle, they sat perfectly still, their red necks stretched up as if expecting mother to come feed them at any moment. Floating in the quiet pool of a rose bowl, surrounded by the delicate pink fronds of their nest, they surprised me again with their fragile beauty.

Can you imagine? Can we even begin to imagine the infinite creativity of the artist who put those flamingoes in the center of those peony blossoms? I guess there are some things we just aren't meant to comprehend. That's what keeps our sense of wonder alive.

Four furry lavender baby birds
Sit back to back on their lily-pad base
Ready to scare intruders off if any
Should find their hiding place.
They patiently wait, day after day,
For a mother who never happens by.
Snug in their pink-frond hideaway,
They silently live and peacefully die.

I marvel, too, at the brief span of their life. The peonies bloom for only a few days in June, each with its little nest of flamingo babies. Then they are gone. What a lavish God we have! And how wise. If such treasures were with us every day, we might become insensitive to the wonders and delights with which our Creator is pleased to surround us. But we can find them only if we become still, and seek them with a childlike heart.

Too much hustle and bustle, too many appointments and meetings, too many assignments and deadlines, will blind our eyes to the daily gifts waiting to surprise us. It was years before I discovered the tiny nestlings snuggled inside the hideaway of fragrant petals.

It won't always be flamingoes hiding in peonies, of course. The surprises come in many ways. I remember the unexpected pools of shadow in circles of light on our lawn during the most recent solar eclipse. It was eerie, like something from a science fiction movie, only better. God's magnificent special effects. Light show. Free. No tickets required. What a neat way for God to say, "Hi, there! I'm thinking about you. And you. And you."

"He makes his sun to shine and his rain to fall on the just and on the unjust," the Bible tells us. The light show wasn't just for Christians, or Jews, or Muslims, or Buddhists. It was for all of us, regardless of what we believe about our maker. Even if we choose not to believe in God, he still believes in us, and continues to woo us with lovely surprises.

Doesn't it just take your breath away when THE original artist flings a great arch of rainbow color across the clouds? And do you remember the frost ferns he painted on your window last winter? The world calls them the work of "Jack Frost", but we know who the real genius is.

Have you ever walked the beach and tried to count the grains of sand? Then you have a small hint of God's immensity. Have you ever picked up a white pebble from the shore and marveled at how smooth it has become? Or wondered how many years of tossing in the ocean it took to make it so beautiful? The next time you find a sand dollar, open it up and ask yourself who hid the five white doves inside it.

Everywhere we turn, in every season of the year, we are surrounded by love notes from our maker. In autumn, the leaves are ablaze with colors we don't even have names for.

They shed an almost iridescent light across the lawns and along the roadsides of our existence. In endless variety, the colors spread across the hilltops and spill down into the valleys like granny afghans draped over sofa backs.

The first snow of winter tells us again of God's infinite variety. Not a single flake is like any other. He has touched them all. Not a single person is like any other. Each is unique in the maker's eyes. Each is precious. You. And you. And you.

The wind blows. We cannot see it, but we have no doubt about its existence. We see the grass ripple before it. We hear the leaves rustle as it goes by. We smell the fragrance of locust tree blossoms carried on the air currents. We feel the freshness of wind on our face. In the wind, God has given us a small picture of what he is like. Unseen, but there. Active. Involved in our lives. Touching us. Bringing daily reminders.

One morning in early spring, I looked out my window and found the trees festooned in light green lace as the new leaves were just starting to open. I stood for a long time drinking in the beauty of it. A few weeks later, the crab apple tree burst into bloom, followed by the hawthorn, with its tiny delicate rosettes. Wild yellow roses came early, with almost a week of golden bounty before the petals fell under the prayed-for rain.

Gifts

Life and death. Winter and summer.
Night and day. Time and timelessness.
Each carries its own special beauty.
Each is a well-planned gift
    from the hand of the One who loves us.
How can we ever say thank you?
Words are so inadequate.

Epitaphs

1994

Tombstones hold a fascination for me. They are full of history—not just names and dates, but clues about what life was like, once upon a time.

I've stood in Pine Hill Cemetery in Morristown, NY, at the grave of a mother I'd never heard of before, and wept for her. Beside her, on smaller stones, were the names and ages of the children she bore and buried. They died at birth, at 18 months of age, two years, five years. I can't imagine losing that many children and still enduring.

History is written in those tombstones. It deplores the childhood illnesses for which vaccines had not yet been invented. It tells of sickness for which the doctor had no remedies. It shows long-suffering parents, sitting by lamplight at the bedside of a sick child, and dying a little inside each time a little one died.

An elaborate stone in the historic cemetery at Longmeadow, Massachusetts, gives comfort to those who would mourn the loss of a child:

They are not lost. They are within the door
that shuts out loss and every hurtful thing.

On the other side of that stone was a poem which says more about the social climate of the times (1871) than many history books do:

The Lord, who many mansions had
Drew near and looked upon a suffering World
Then, pitying, spake, Give me the little lad

In strength renewed and glorious beauty clad
I'll bring him with me when I come again.

This community, along with others in the whole eastern half of the country, had just come through a bloody Civil War. Many families had lost fathers, husbands, sons and brothers in the conflict. Their only real comfort in the face of such unspeakable tragedy was a serene faith in the goodness of God.

Again and again that faith is spelled out in stone, in that cemetery and others. This epitaph was on the tombstone of a 75 year old man who had died in 1831:

He had fixed the anchor of his hope
Upon the rock of endless ages
And feared not to die

Nearby, the stone of a woman who had died in 1810 said simply:

Believe, and look with triumph in the tomb

Another woman, who died in 1804 at the age of 31, had this engraved upon her stone:

Cease my beloved to complain
My dust returns to dust again
But my immortal soul is gone
To put eternal glory on

This triumphant tone is echoed on the stone of an 89 year old man who was buried in Longmeadow in 1808:

My flesh shall slumber in the ground
Til the last trumpet's joyful sound
Then burst the chains with sweet surprise
And in my Savior's image rise.

Other epitaphs are purely philosophical. This one from 1807 is a good example:

Some hearty friend shall drop his tear
On our dry bones and say
"These once were strong as mine appear,
and mine must be as they"
Thus shall our mouldering members teach
What everyone should learn
For dust and ashes loudest preach
Man's infinite concern.

Can you imagine what it would cost to have that engraved on a tombstone today? Another one in the philosophical vein was given me by Bernard Hill. He found it while doing genealogical research. The stone marks the grave of one of his ancestors, Abraham Dewey, who died in 1792. It says simply:

Death is a debt to nature due,
Which I have paid and so must you.

Walking in old cemeteries and reading the history in them can be a fascinating pastime for you, too. Be sure to take a notebook and pencil to copy down the strange and interesting things you'll discover there.

Memory Walk

I walk among the myrtle,
Like a lovely blanket spread
O'er the silent resting places
Of the long-forgotten dead.
And my fingers trace the letters
Carved so long ago in stone
Where the storms have worn the edges
And the moss has overgrown.

As my fingers "read" the message,
It makes me stop to think
How the words they left behind them
Have become an unseen link
To those stalwart men and women
Whose laughter, toil and tears
Have forged a splendid heritage
That's lasted through the years.

Today, WE'RE etching history
On stone and glass and steel,
That somewhere down the centuries
Someone may read, and feel
Our loves and joys and struggles,
Our laughter, pain and fears,
And feel a sense of kinship—
A link that spans the years.

Prune

2000

I hear on the news
    the "powers that be"
        have opted to banish the prune.
For "prune's" not attractive—
    It turns people off.
        We'll sing it by some other tune.
And so they've renamed it—
"Dried Plum" they've proclaimed it,
    tho' its properties all stay the same.
Dried plum juice, they think,
    is what we should drink.
What a fuss to make over a name!

A prune is a prune, whatever they call it,
    So sweet and tender and mild.
It's fit for a king or a queen on a throne,
    as well as a mother and child.
But a word thusly banished,
    will also make vanished
        a term that is lucidly clear,
    for no more can we say,
        when they soak half a day,
"Hurry up! You'll be all pruney, dear."

Pruning

2000

O, well. At least I trust the arbiters of things semantic will not banish the other meaning of the word "prune". For that's what I've been doing—pruning plants and trees and shrubs around the yard. The red maple on the corner was spreading its branches so far out it almost interfered with the ability to see oncoming traffic.

The silver maple's branches draped down in graceful profusion until they could brush the hair of people walking by on the sidewalk.

It seems as if all the vegetation around us is growing in generous abundance this year. The sugar maples are loaded heavily with clusters of seeds. The gray birch bends to caress Don's head when he mows the lawn. Even the rhubarb, now wilted from the heat, produced extravagantly this spring and the tiger lilies have more buds than I have ever seen at one time. Weeds, of course, have thrived along with everything else. But I enjoy seeing so much bounty, I don't mind the work it brings.

That said, I'd better get back to my pruning. I like to do it in the cool of the day, either before the sun gets too hot for comfort, or when it's low in the west and the sky makes a colorful backdrop for looking up through the branches and deciding which really need to come down.

House plants need pruning, too. I have a big jade plant that I inherited about 15 years ago. It grew too top heavy and bent down over the sides of the planter. It seemed every time the cat walked by it, some leaves or a small branch would break off. Eventually, the big stems started to disintegrate and I ended up starting several new plants with cuttings I saved. It pays to prune before the plant suffers such total collapse. Now I have several pots of jade, looking healthy and thriving.

In some ways, I hate to cut back such wildly enthusiastic growth. But experience tells me it is better, not only for sight distance and for the people who walk underneath our trees, but it is better for the tree or plant to have excessive growth trimmed back. Trees not only look better, they are less subject to storm damage.

People are a lot like trees. We develop enthusiasms and spread ourselves around liberally until the slightest adverse wind sets us dashing about wildly. Weakened by the whipping of the wind, we easily break beneath the weight of an ice storm. The storms of life are not all in the weather realm, as most of us already know.

Sometimes, to protect ourselves from the ravages of adverse circumstances, we need to prune our activities and interests. Time management experts call it prioritizing. What is most important for us to do? You notice, I didn't ask what is most urgent. Often the urgent things that demand our attention are not the most important if viewed in the long-term perspective of life goals and philosophies.

Right now, it is a beautiful sunny day. I could be outside doing some more pruning, and I really would enjoy that. But I have made a choice to finish this column instead. Someone else can do the pruning if I don't get it all done, but no one else will write this column for me.

I tell you all this because I realize that the pruning we have to undergo in life can sometimes be unwelcome and painful. We are likely to ask "Why?" when this occurs. But just as a tree does better and even looks better, at least the following season, so it may take time for us to appreciate the good that our being pruned may do for us.

In the meantime, we can be thankful for the Gardener who prunes us, even if we don't understand the need for it at the time. And we can look with expectation for the improvements, even if they aren't obvious right away.

First Impressions

1994

There are three little stories I'd like to tell you. At first they may not seem related at all, but wait...

* * * * *

Recently the mail brought yet another sales sheet purporting to offer sensational bargains. One of the "bargains" was a 12-roll pack of bathroom tissue with "280 two-ply sheets" at a very reasonable price. Trouble is, by the time we got there, that sale item was gone, and the store graciously substituted a big name brand 12-roll pack for the same money. I checked it out later and found these rolls contained only 170 two-ply sheets. That's less than half the volume of product for the same "special" price.

* * * * *

A young man and woman we once knew were having a very difficult time adjusting to their new roles as husband and wife. They found compatibility in many areas, but there was an uneasy frustration and sense of inferiority each felt when it came to decision making. After struggling with this problem for several months, they finally went to a marriage counselor, who was able to pinpoint the trouble very quickly.

It seems when the husband was unsure about something, or trying to decide on a course of action, he was very quiet, giving it a lot of thought. She, on the other hand, talked incessantly about all the possibilities, exploring all the angles verbally. When she had arrived at the best solution, in her judgement, she became quiet, savoring the satisfaction of having found the right answer. Meantime he had arrived at his own decision mentally, and became relaxed and talkative.

Because she was used to being quiet when the decision had been made, she assumed his initial quietness meant he already had it figured out, and that made her feel inferior when it happened all the time. Because he was used to talking in a relaxed fashion after figuring something out and his wife started talking right away, he assumed she already had the answer and it made him feel inferior. Each was surprised to learn the other viewed them as having superior wisdom. Both were pleased at finding it was just a communication difference, and the problem vanished.

* * * * *

Years ago, our family made friends with two single ladies who attended the same church. Invitations to Sunday dinner were a frequent occurrence among a variety of different friends in those days. These particular two friends seemed a bit offish when they were both invited at the same time. But gradually they seemed to forget whatever it was that made them uncomfortable together and eventually became the best of friends. We found out years later that each had perceived the other as cold and unfriendly, maybe even stuck up. In reality, each was shy and retiring, unable to make the first move toward being friendly.

* * * * *

These stories all illustrate our need to recognize that things aren't always what they seem. We could save ourselves much frustration, unhappiness, loneliness, bad bargains, and embarrassment if we could learn to take a good look at the people and circumstances in our lives.

Some rules of thumb might even be helpful. When it comes to buying merchandise, the old advice, "Let the buyer beware!" is still a good rule to follow.

When it comes to people, giving them the benefit of the doubt is a good practice. We were taught the Golden Rule as children and it's just as valid today as it was thousands of years ago when the first person to voice it set a standard for the rest of us.

Look Beyond

You'll find that things aren't always what they seem.
A "bargain" may be only "bait and switch",
A terrifying fall may be a dream.
The trick is, understanding which is which.

A person may seem snooty in our eyes,
And yet, behind that cold reserve we'll find
A friendliness we'd never realize
If we ourselves remained aloof and "blind".

So stretch your heart. Come, open wide its door
And welcome in the lonely and distressed.
You'll find your life enriched, and so much more-
For you, and all you welcome, will be blest.

Olympic Games

July 1996

Pomp and circumstance, artistry and fantasy combined to form a vast and colorful extravaganza for the opening ceremonies of the 1996 Summer Olympics in Atlanta. The choreography was superb. The costuming was elegant, colorful and fanciful. Lively music drew the capacity crowd into the drama and excitement of the evening.

Whatever else the United States may be good at doing, it takes the gold in glamor, innovation and showmanship. But the organizers didn't show much sensitivity to the needs of the competing athletes, keeping them standing around for hours and not even lighting the Olympic torch until well after midnight. I'll bet those athletes didn't keep those kinds of hours when in training. But they still were expected to be up and ready for competition the next day.

To their credit, they did very well, despite adverse conditions which included not only loss of sleep but excessive heat, an extra challenge for those from northern climes.

I find myself getting all tense and breathless when I watch the swimming and rowing competitions. I wouldn't make a very good athlete, not when I get tired out just watching others go through their paces. Still, it's fun to see the gymnasts perform feats that are humanly impossible. There is a grace and beauty to their tumbling routines, parallel bar exercises and balance beam ballets that is truly exhilarating.

But then, I step back from this world of competition, this glitter and energy that seem bigger than life, even on a small screen. I ask myself, Why? Why do we go to such lengths to prove who is the best swimmer in the world? Or the fastest runner? Or the bicyclist with the greatest skill and endurance? Why?

Anthropologists would tell us these games provide a forum for release of natural aggressiveness and that the intense competition and the hard won victories are effective substitutes for political aggressiveness that might otherwise erupt in the violence of wars. If this is true, we should see fewer and fewer wars. But that isn't the case.

Social scientists say these games draw nations together and help them to look at each other as friendly competitors rather than enemies. It's true that individual athletes from competing countries may build close friendships. But does that really affect the way the political institutions of those countries view each other? It seems more likely that the political systems affect the individuals and their attitudes about the other athletes.

In pre-event interviews with individual athletes, we often hear the phrase, "I wouldn't be here if I didn't think I could win the gold." Is that just a psyching-up device the athletes use to help themselves into a winning frame of mind? Or is it a matter of self-centered arrogance? Are they really saying, "If I can't be top dog, I'm not interested in playing the game." If everyone had that attitude, the Olympics would face sudden death.

Only a small percentage of the competitors walk away with gold. I'm much more impressed by the athletes who say, "I'll do my very best. My teammates are depending on me." Or, "I'm just so proud to be chosen to represent my country. I don't want to disappoint them."

The arrogant ones *need* to be bested before they become crippled with "hardening of the attitudes." I love to see the humble ones win, the ones who by discipline, persistence and hard work have climbed to the top of their sport, but do not feel the need to gloat. Did you see Angel give her medal to a teammate who was sidelined by a battle with cancer? "Blessed are the meek, for they shall inherit the earth."

After the Glory

Games are just that—
    Games.
They may be surrounded with
    glitter and glamor and glory,
        but after the stadium's closed
            and crowds have gone home
                and no one remembers your name,
It's still just a game.

Life is what's real—
    Life!
Where we are surrounded by
    challenges, problems and strife,
        where we have a chance to
            write a new page of the story.
After our lifework is done,
    and at last we go home,
        it will no longer matter
            how many the games we have won
                nor how many medals we wear.
All that will matter then
    is only the joy we will know
        when the great Creator of all
            gives gold for our obedience,
                silver for our selflessness
                    and bronze for dependability.
Then we will know that life
    and work
        and game
            were only the training arena.
Here, in the winners' circle,
    the Creator calls us by name!

Roads

August 1994

"A little white road winds over the hill. My feet they must follow, they cannot be still...". This pleasant little song was a favorite of my childhood and seems to describe summer this year. It sets me to thinking about roads. Many of you will think the picture of a white road is unrealistic. But the roads of my childhood *were* white—the paved roads at least.

When I was young, the state highways were paved with concrete. It was poured in sections about thirty feet long with space between the sections to allow for expansion and contraction of temperature changes. There was also expansion space between lanes. These spaces were filled with tar, which also changed with the weather. The resulting surface sang a rhythmic ka-thunk, ka-thunk, ka-thunk as the car rolled over the tarred joints. Small sections of those concrete highways still exist and still sing ka-thunk, ka-thunk as cars pass. But the song is faster today to match the speeded-up pace of life and travel.

Back roads of my early memories were mostly dirt roads, packed down by travel. They were always higher in the middle between the wheel tracks and often became muddy and full of ruts after rain. The better side roads were paved with macadam, a crushed stone and asphalt mixture, which was developed in the early 1800s by Scottish inventor John L. McAdam. I didn't know that then, of course. But I liked the smooth surface and the way the roads were made slightly higher in the middle so the rain would run off into ditches.

The white concrete, gray macadam and brown dirt roads aren't the only colors of roads that beckon people to travel.

Near Morristown, N.Y., there is pink pavement! Apparently they made the concrete surface using crushed red granite from nearby quarries. In North River, the road that goes up to the garnet mine is paved with dark crushed stone that's full of sparkles. This is the kind of stone that surrounds the garnet deposits and is a by-product of garnet mining, put to good use.

Today's newer highways are smooth ribbons of blacktop, an improved version of the basic macadam road. Giant machines can now chew up old road surfaces, mix them with additional asphalt, and roll out a thick new layer of highway all in one operation. Within hours a new road appears where an old, cracked, pot-holed road had been. Bright, reflective, long-lasting paints are used to apply the yellow center lines and white fog-line edges. Almost like magic we have safety engineered highways that can take us almost anywhere we want to go.

People remind me of roads—different colors, different widths, different lengths and going different places. Some folks walk with a cane or walker and when they pass it almost sounds like the song of the concrete road—ka-thunk, ka-thunk, ka-thunk.

Some folks kick up dust like a car hurrying down a dirt road in dry weather, and some fling mud like a car stuck in a rut in the rain. Others give us pleasant surprises like the road made of pink granite. Still others sparkle even from dark places in their lives, just like the sparkly road that leads to the garnet mine.

Some live orderly lives, smooth and gentle like a new black-top surface, staying within the boundaries marked by the bright paint of custom and tradition. They enjoy a life that's safe and predictable. Others are adventurous and prefer the by-ways, even if there are dangerous pot holes and broken edges and no road markings. They just want to see what's around the next bend or over the next hill.

Variety is so exciting—in roads, or in people. Enjoy.

Wanderlust

The lure of the highway beckons.
There are so many things to see,
So many places I've never been
That seem to be calling me.

So many paths I have yet to explore,
So many hills yet to climb,
So many discoveries 'round each bend
Just waiting to tickle my mind.

For a path or a road or a highway
Are inviting, are bidding us come
To follow the call of the open road
In the wind and the rain and the sun!

Mementos

June 1994

"I LOVE YOU", the caption on the picture says. A fuzzy creature, looking like a cross between a bear cub and a mouse, clings to a branch and gazes fondly at a ladybug resting there. It's silly, of course. But it says what needs to be said:

We don't need to be alike to cherish each other. We don't have to be biologically correct to have feelings and express them. Love and sex are not synonymous. We all thrive on hearing those three little reassuring words, and feeling the warmth and caring that give them life. That's really quite a lot for one silly little picture to say.

The "I LOVE YOU" picture was painted for me by a friend several years ago. She moved far away, but I always think of her when I see it.

On the other side of the door is an entirely different kind of painting. Small in size and set in a dark wood frame, it shows a weathered elderly gentleman, dressed in garb from another time and another place. His patient eyes, looking out from under a broad hat brim, have seen many decades of life's toils and pleasures, disappointments and satisfactions.

Clenched in the left corner of his mouth is the stem of a long, curved pipe, which he is in the process of lighting. The glow from the match sets off the deep wrinkles around his eyes and forehead. Plainly, his life has not been one of ease. A sparse gray stubble covers the contours of his jaw.

At his right elbow can be seen the curved arm of a seat, such as might have been found in an old world pub, and a half filled glass stands on the table before him. No artist's name can be seen, but it resembles work of the old Dutch masters.

The man-in-the-pub painting was among the possessions of an elderly gentleman who lived with us for a time and who had no near kin to claim his meager belongings. His presence in our lives tested our patience and enriched us with tales of local history. He was one of the agents God used in shaping us.

On the wall to my right is a pull-out poster from *Writer's Digest Magazine*. It says, "Do not disturb. Writer at work." It brings me back to the present, of course, and to the task at hand. I tell you all this because I believe the things with which people surround themselves tell a lot about who they are.

The poster reminds me of what I am still becoming, one column at a time, one poem at a time.

If you want to understand more about who you are, look around you at the things you save and treasure. You may discover some very revealing things you hadn't thought of in that way before.

I look with an analytical eye at the possessions that fill my house. My curiosity, my thirst for knowledge and my love for reading have filled shelf after shelf with books. My thrifty Scottish ancestry has made me a saver of anything that might someday be useful. The meagerness we knew growing up in the years of the Great Depression, has worked to make us accumulators, surrounding ourselves with things our parents could never hope to own.

Our lives span worlds so completely different that it is hard for our grandchildren to understand what life was like for us at their age. They cannot comprehend life before television. They can't imagine being part of a family that had no car, no electricity, no running water, no telephone, no radio, no video games.

Even the generation between us and our grandchildren can scarcely believe how life was before Social Security, before Medicare and Medicaid, ball-point pens and shopping malls, Kleenex and golf courses.

And the generation starting school now will not know how we ever survived without personal computers, CD encyclopedias, spell checkers, hand-held calculators for use on math regents, cellular phones and e-mail.

We need some of the pictures and keepsakes to remind us of who we are, where we came from, and even in what direction we are going. Someone has said if you want to know what your real priorities are, ask yourself what you'd like to accomplish before you die if you knew you had only one more year to live. Now THAT is a question to make anyone pause and think, to put their own goals and activities and accumulations into perspective.

Short Time—Long Vision

I look around, and suddenly I see,
with keener vision,
all the things I want to be,
And all the things I want to do
while I am here—
whether that be half a century,
or just a single year.

I look around and, marveling,
I find the things I have collected
have collected me.
They shaped my life, but also made me blind
to much that is more precious than mere things.
And I am sad. But I am also glad,
for time still waits for me
to stop my dallying and fly—
into a future that is better than today.

Changeable

1992

"Fire and ice and marshmallows". That's how we often referred to one of our small sons. His temperament was so changeable that he'd be fired with anger or indignation one minute, cool and aloof the next, and loving and cuddly a few minutes later.

We've often remarked how different each child is. One was the soul of generosity, one an outgoing people-person, one the personification of gentleness, one a crusader for justice, one a perfectionist, one a timid introvert masking a witty mischief.

"How can children be so different when they're raised in the same family under the influence of the same parents?" We've often heard people ask that question. But it's really not so strange. The truth is, the parents *aren't* the same parents with the second child they were with the first. And they aren't the same with the third or fourth as they were with the second. Each parent, growing in knowledge, understanding and experience, subtly changes in attitudes and behavior. These changes show in how we interact with each successive child.

Not having had previous training in how to be parents, except for observing our own parents in action, we tend to be up tight at first about doing everything just right.

I once babysat for a couple who had their new baby on such a rigid schedule that they let her cry for two hours because it wasn't her scheduled time to eat yet. By then she'd be too exhausted to eat her fill. She'd go to sleep almost as soon as the first warm milk hit her stomach. Then she'd be hungry again in short order. Finally she'd cry herself to sleep again only to have her well-meaning parents disturb her rest to pick her up and feed her—because the clock said it was time.

These people were well educated, but they had made the mistake of listening to "experts" rather than to experienced parents. When our first child was still trying to teach us the rudiments of common sense care, I asked the doctor question after question about what to do in this or that circumstance and he simply said, "Don't ask me; ask a woman who's raised several children. She knows what works."

So I asked my mother and I asked Don's mother and I got two quite different answers. Fortunately, babies are adaptable. They'll suffer through lots of misdirected good intentions and still think their parents are the best parents in the world. It's the only way we managed to fake it through. But we did learn. We listened to others, and we also learned to listen to our own instincts. We changed. The way we interacted with our children changed. And today they are about as far from carbon copies of each other as you could get.

I see a difference, not only between the children in a family, but also differences within individuals—like our fire-and-ice-and-marshmallows son. Personalities have different facets. We may be tense, easy going, adventurous, or timid. Sometimes we let off steam. Other times we're patient and tolerant. Unsettling? Yes, but it keeps life interesting.

If we are alive and growing and paying attention to life's lessons, we don't remain the same people we once were. And it's a good thing. We can all stand a little improvement.

I know a young lady who used to be shy. She had no boy friends in high school; the boys didn't seem to know she existed. The few who paid attention to her didn't appeal to her at all. Some friends arranged a date for her with an out-of-area young man, and they were married within a few months. She now has a large circle of friends, a fine family, and a healthy self image. Different facets of her personality have developed and flowered. It is a pleasure to watch such a metamorphosis—like watching a caterpillar become a butterfly.

Then there was the skinny kid who looked like Ichabod Crane in Irving's famous story. Athletes were the center of attention at his school, and macho just wasn't in his nature, so he became a class clown. Today he's a respected professional man and a published author.

Another lad, husky, hard working and patriotic, had his life suddenly changed by an enemy bullet. It never occurred to him to give up. Instead of an active body, he developed active mind and hands to help others.

Today is a good time to take a look at our lives and assess how we're doing, to be thankful for the good things and to look for ways of overcoming the not-so-good.

Facets

The oyster overcomes the grain of sand
Surrounding it with softly shining pearl.
One woodsman sees a maple tree diseased;
Another sees a handsome, rich-grained burl.

In all the trials and blessings of our life
The hurtful and the lovely are entwined,
Giving our days a richness and a grace
To strengthen us and make us wise and kind.

Only beware, lest bitterness creep in
And with its tendrils twist the way we see.
For what might well have been a boon, disguised,
Could turn to ashes, dust and misery.

Each person is a many-splendored jewel
With facets to be cut for luster, fine.
Take care you do not chip or scratch these gems,
But polish them with love and make them shine!

Up, Up and Away

September 1993

"Let me tell you about my operation!"

Don't you just cringe when someone says that? So I won't bore you with the details. Actually, I don't know the details yet. I'm still waiting for "the ride down the hall."

But let me tell you why I need surgery. The doctor says if you have to have a broken ankle, it's much better to have an interesting story to go with it. And I have a broken ankle.

We spent Labor Day Weekend at the Gatineau, Quebec, Hot Air Balloon Festival. What an experience! Don and I worked with the ground crew for "Spirit", a rainbow-striped balloon piloted by Larry Fortin of Kingston, Rhode Island. Fully inflated, "Spirit" holds 90,000 cubic feet of air and towers 80 feet into the morning sky!

When we first arrive at the festival park, the balloon field is dotted with chase vehicles unloading equipment. The pilots have just come from their 5:30 a.m. pre-flight briefing. Baskets are set on the ground and envelopes are pulled from heavy canvas bags and spread out over the grass in line with the wind direction. Some crew members mount the upright frame to the gondola, others attach control lines or fasten the crown into place with hooks and velcro. Spectators flock into the fenced-off viewing areas. Fare paying passengers come out to their assigned launch sites and watch with interest all the preparations.

Lines are secured. Burners are mounted in the frame. They WHOOOOSH and tall flames leap into the air. All systems are ready. It's time to inflate. The big hoop at the lower end of the balloon is held open by two crew members, and a powerful fan begins filling the envelope with air. Flowing nylon panels undulate like ocean waves as the colorful balloons grow larger and larger. One helper holds the crown rope straight out to help stabilize the balloon and keep it from rolling sideways as it fills.

Now the envelope is full of air. The basket is tipped on its side and the burners aimed straight ahead inside the balloon. Short blasts of gas-flame heat the air in the balloon until it expands and the balloon starts to stand up. What a sight! Everywhere we look, tall balloons strain at their ropes, anxious to be up and away. Passengers climb quickly into the basket, now upright. Once more the flames leap up, the lines are released—and we're off!

"Spirit" shoots upward like a homesick angel. We look back at the launch field where other balloons still swell and bob, straining at their ropes. We drift slowly to the south, across the Ottawa River. West of us stand the stately Parliament buildings, looking like intricate miniatures from this altitude. The Ottawa and Gatineau rivers and the Rideau River and canal spread over the scenery like pools and streaks of silver. Everything is so beautiful!

We float on across the city, the suburbs and the fields and woods beyond. Our chase vehicle can be seen plainly on the road below. The pilot communicates with the ground crew by two-way radio. There's a good field for landing, the pilot decides. He turns on the burners to lift us above cows and horses in a pasture—balloons sometimes make them skittish—then pulls skillfully on vents to begin letting the hot air out of the envelope so we can descend.

"When we land," the pilot tells us, "keep your knees flexed as if you were skiing. Crouch down in the basket to lower the center of gravity. Put one hand on an upright, like this, and one hand through the low hand-loop inside the basket."

We all follow instructions—almost—and all land safely—almost.

The emergency room staff at Ottawa's Riverside Hospital is friendly and helpful. "This can't be treated conservatively," the orthopedic surgeon says. "I can repair it for you tonight, or you can go home, if you prefer. But be sure you have the necessary surgery."

So here I am, with time on my hands, appreciating the morphine pump but having trouble focusing my eyes *or* my mind.

My brother says, "It beats all what some folks will do for a story." My son-in-law, who is part of the chase crew, gives me a line to open this week's column with—"Aside from that, Mrs. Lincoln, how did you like the play?"

Breathless Adventure

But I'd go again in a heartbeat
For there's nothing can quite compare
With the rush of anticipation
And the tug of the morning air
Or the marvelous burst of color
As the "Spirit" stretches high
Pushing its rainbow brilliance
Into the morning sky!

On With the Show

September 1993

"The show must go on!"

This dictum has propelled many a project forward when the going was rough, or when progress seemed almost impossible. It kept me going last week when I wrote my column for the paper through a haze of pre-op sedation and found it almost impossible to concentrate on putting words together. I'd write a few, then rest my eyes and brain, then reread to pick up my drift and add a few more words. Don came into my hospital room and found me sound asleep, sitting up, with pen poised over notebook.

I tell you this because I think adversity is often seen as a good excuse to do nothing. I'm sure all my readers would have been understanding if I had missed a week. But I find the self discipline needed to keep going is a valuable tool for building strength and endurance.

When I was a very small child, my older brother and I went sliding down the hill behind our house, enjoying the winter fun. Inevitably, I found myself at the bottom of the hill on one trip, too cold and tired to climb back up again. David wasn't big enough to pull the sled up the hill with me on it. There was nothing to do but to put one foot in front of the other and keep going until we were back to the warmth of the house.

When I was eight, we walked to vacation Bible school every day for two weeks, and walked home again at noon. Now this wasn't just a block down the street. The church was over a mile away with two long hills to go down in the morning and two very long, very steep hills to climb back to home in the heat of the day. Many a time I would have liked to stop somewhere for a drink of water and a rest. But I just had to keep on keeping on.

I don't remember these incidents as times of deprivation or parental neglect, but as times where the circumstances of my life called upon me to extend myself beyond my normal limits. They were times that built character and endurance. Today, that endurance is helping me weather the inconvenience and discomfort, the strain and the pain of a broken ankle.

Sometimes I think we make life too easy for our children. We cart them here and there in expensive cars run on expensive fuels so they can participate in expensive activities or enjoy expensive entertainments. Instead of learning to be self reliant and persistent, they are learning a subtle message that the world owes them a living. They grow up thinking they deserve to be treated like royalty. Then, because they have not struggled nor sacrificed to earn the advantages they have, they tend to devalue those advantages and to become dissatisfied with life.

Persistence can be exhausting. Determination in the face of adversity is hard. Struggle is not fun. But these things are all necessary to build character and personal satisfaction.

The show must go on. Not for the sake of the show. Not for the sake of the audience. Not for the sake of the income. Not for the sake of what others may think. The show must go on for the sake of the growth and development, the stamina and the integrity of the individual involved in the struggle.

I write this column not for the publicity, not for the sake of my "fans", not for the paycheck, but because the self discipline of writing it every week helps me to grow in my writing skills. It helps me to appreciate my past. It helps me to think deeply about the present and the future. It gives me an opportunity to share insights, experiences, discoveries, hopes and dreams with others. It widens my circle of friends.

Worth it!

There is nothing in life worth having
If it isn't worth time and thought,
If it isn't worth struggle and heartache,
If the getting has cost us naught.

For the only things of value
Are earned by struggle and pain,
Through toil and deprivation,
By trying again and again.

There are love and wisdom and honor,
There are friendships and character too,
That are worth the work and trials
To help make dreams to come true.

Bedtime Stories

1995

With a chuckle, Don handed me a small book to read. I glanced at the title, "Politically Correct Bedtime Stories," and groaned. Why would anyone want to waste money on a title like that?, I thought aloud.

"Oh, I didn't spend that much," he said. "I found it at a used book store."

I glanced at the brief critiques one finds on book jackets and groaned again.

"It's hard to believe that James Finn Garner could improve upon perfection--but he has!" said the first one. It was attributed to Hans Christian Andersen. (Does that give you a clue?)

The next one supposedly came from The Brothers Grimm, who were quoted as commenting thus: "We were fighting between ourselves to see who would read it first."

The last was extrapolated from the time-honored story teller, Aesop. "These stories are fables for our times," it said.

According to the jacket, the book is categorized as humor. And it certainly does highlight and exaggerate some of the trends we see. But in doing that, it paints a surrealistic picture of a society gone wrong. Like a court jester, Garner spins tales of truth couched in ridiculous hyperbole that brings forth laughter. We laugh to keep from squirming.

In this one small volume, thirteen familiar children's classic stories are chopped up, punched around, kicked and pummeled, rearranged, stretched, twisted and garbled. Only the names of the main characters remain the same, to punish the non-innocent.

For example, look at what happened to Little Red Riding Hood in these looking-glass pages: "One day her mother asked her to take a basket of fresh fruit and mineral water to her grandmother's house—not because this was womyn's work, mind you, but because the deed was generous and helped engender a feeling of community."

Further on in the tale, at her grandmother's house, we find this "politically correct" exchange: "'Grandma, what big teeth you have!' The wolf said, 'I am happy with who I am and what I am,' and leaped out of bed. He grabbed Red Riding Hood in his claws, intent on devouring her. Red Riding Hood screamed, not out of alarm at the wolf's apparent tendency toward cross-dressing, but because of his willful invasion of her personal space."

You get the idea. Then there is the humorous story of The Emperor's New Clothes. You'll recall in the original that the vain emperor was duped by an unscrupulous tailor into believing that he would be the first to wear this new, fine fabric, which he couldn't see, but dared not admit he couldn't. When the time came for him to show off his new clothes in public, all his subjects went along with the ruse, not daring to call the emperor stupid. Except for one small boy, not yet old enough to be devious. Let's pick up the altered version there.

"As the emperor marched his pale, bloated, patriarchal carcass down the street, everyone loudly oohed and ahed at his beautiful new clothes. All except one small boy, who shouted: 'The emperor is naked!' The parade stopped. The emperor paused. A hush fell over the crowd, until one quick-thinking peasant shouted: 'No, he isn't. The emperor is merely endorsing a clothing-optional lifestyle!' A cheer went up from the crowd, and the throngs stripped off their clothes and danced in the sun, as Nature had intended."

The book's 79 pages of print are peppered with gender bias backlash, anti-patriarchal barbs, adult innuendoes, jabs against imperialism and acid remarks about people who misuse the environment, all wrapped in off-the-wall, pun-in-chic antics.

Let's peek at the Three Little Pigs, who have escaped the wolf and are gathered in the brick house: "This time in response, the pigs sang songs of solidarity and wrote letters of protest to the United Nations. By now the wolf was getting angry at the pigs' refusal to see the situation from the carnivore's point of view, so he huffed and puffed, and huffed and puffed, then grabbed his chest and fell over dead from a massive heart attack brought on from eating too many fatty foods."

So much for politically correct eating habits. And of course we can't let children grow up thinking that bigger or older is necessarily stronger or better. Here, younger becomes "least chronologically accomplished", larger size becomes "physical-intimidation prerogative", filthy and smelly becomes "dirt-accomplished and odor-enhanced" and short becomes "vertically challenged." In the story of Chicken Little we read, "(It should be mentioned here that the name 'Little' was a family name, and not a derogatory, size-biased nickname. It was only by sheer coincidence that Chicken Little was also of shorter-than-average height.)"

You may laugh if you wish. It's always good to laugh at our own foibles. There are, unfortunately, people who enjoy making others uncomfortable, who get their jollies by bouncing put-downs off their hapless victims. But it's also unfortunate that we have people who think they have to bend over backwards to avoid any reference to size or gender or ethnicity that might possibly be construed as derogatory. Their verbal juggling is ridiculous.

I tell you all this because I think we tend to take ourselves too seriously. We need to loosen up and have a little fun—at our own expense. Those who laugh at the plight of others have much to learn about life. But those who cannot laugh at themselves are miserable indeed.

Let's see...what "politically correct" terminology could I poke at myself in jest? To begin with, I am chronologically advantaged (from my point of view), being multiply-decaded. I'm also girth-augmented, gender-impaired (in a patriarchal society), humor-enhanced How's that for being honesty-integrated?

Politically Correct

Oh, let us be, politically,
Correct in terminology,
Defining life in useful ways
While walking in an
 eggshell daze, to keep from
Stepping on the toes
Of gender-biased folks,
 and those who can't abide
A little fun, but to their
Novel speech rules run to
Find alternative ways to say
That black and white are not
 quite gray, but must,
Instead, be tone-diminished.
And work not done is semi-
 finished. Along this same
And devious track, they find
That night is not just black,
But actually is light-impaired
And bad dreams never make you
Scared; they simply leave you
Rest-deprived, angst-enhanced
 and shorter-lived. Enough!
I say, enough already. My
Equilibrium grows unsteady.
My mind is spinning
 like a top. Forsooth,
In truth, I have to stop.

Life's Hard Lessons

1995

Have I ever told you about my childhood escapades? There are a few that really stand out, three in particular, and Maggie (name changed to protect the innocent?) was part of them.

When I was in kindergarten, I took my little sister Dottie to school with me one morning. Schools were smaller and more laid back about visitors in those days. It was sort of the forerunner of show-and-tell. I brought my sister to show her off. It made me feel big and important to be her guardian and protector. And it probably made me feel a little superior to those who didn't have a sister to show off.

On the way home, Maggie ran ahead and hid behind some bushes. When we came along, she jumped out and scared Dottie. Now that made me mad and I started to chase Maggie, but I couldn't hold onto Dottie and catch Maggie at the same time. So I picked up a stone, determined to frighten Maggie away if she tried it again.

She did. And I let fly with that stone, planning to zing it past her ear and frighten her away. Well, my aim was a little off. The stone hit the pavement in front of her and bounced up and smacked her right in the middle of the forehead! Today they'd call that a Freudian slip. Whatever they called it then, it accomplished two things. It sent Maggie howling home—no more scaring Dottie. And it sent me home trembling in my boots. I just knew Maggie's mother would be right over and probably kill me.

I stumbled over myself to get the whole story told to Mother before the avenging monster arrived. Mother told me

I knew better than to throw stones, for any reason, and promptly took me to the woodshed where she applied the stick of correction to my seat of learning. Then she dealt with my obvious fear, assuring me that Maggie's mother would not harm me.

I flew to my room to hide. Lunch held no appeal for me. It wasn't long before I heard the clump of angry steps on the porch and voices buzzing below me. I strained to hear, but couldn't make out what they were saying. After awhile I thought I heard the steps go away. But I waited, anyway, thinking she was probably just trying to trick me into coming down where she could get her hands on me.

Finally, Mother called me to come down. It was nearly time to go back to school for the afternoon. I dreaded going. I was sure the teacher would take one look at Maggie and give me another spanking. But I had to go. Very reluctantly.

Maggie was there already. I glanced her way and saw a big purple egg, like a third eye staring back at me. I don't think I learned a thing in school that day. But I learned a lot outside of school. I learned not to throw stones. I learned my mother could handle even the most desperate situation. And I learned not to trust Maggie. Well, almost...

Winter came, and Maggie and I were friends again, often walking to and from school together. One day as we were coming by the railing that borders the Catholic Church lawn, Maggie pointed to the frost on the round iron handrail. "Stick your tongue on that," she said. "It tastes different."

I guess I didn't want Maggie to know anything I didn't know, so I tasted that frost. I was about to tell her I didn't taste anything different about it, when I discovered I couldn't talk. My tongue was stuck fast to that cold iron rail! Maggie laughed a heartless, wicked laugh and ran for home.

Enraged and panicky, I tried again to free myself. I had visions of losing my tongue right there. One more desperate pull and I was running for home, my tongue sore and bleeding. Mother comforted me and told me my tongue would have melted the frost if I had only waited a few more seconds. Boy, was I mad at Maggie!

Spring came. Maggie and I were friends again. Sometimes I wondered if there was anything else she knew that I didn't know. Walking home from school one day, we passed this lovely bed of tulips with a little fence around them.

"O, let's pick some and take them home to our mothers," Maggie said. I didn't think that was right and I told her so. But Maggie insisted the people who owned them wouldn't mind. They wouldn't even miss them. How could she know that? I wondered. Then I realized there *were* a lot of them. Maybe they wouldn't miss a few.

Maggie was already picking some. I was aghast--she had some big red ones. They'd be sure to miss those! I reached over and picked one of the more plentiful yellow ones and said that would be enough. Maggie jeered at my timidity, and marched proudly home with her bounty. I almost wished I had gotten one of the prettier ones for my mother. It wasn't fair that Maggie's mother got the best ones.

Mother was not thrilled. In fact she even discussed the possibility of another trip to the woodshed. Then she thought of a better way to teach me the lesson. Stealing is wrong, no matter what Maggie said. Mother told me so, and she told me I'd have to take the tulip back and return it to the woman who lived by the flower garden.

I was mortified. I asked her if she'd go with me. She wouldn't. I had taken the tulip without her help. I could return it without her help. So I went. Reluctantly. I knocked on the big dark door, hoping no one would hear and I could just put the ugly tulip back in the flower bed and say I'd returned it.

No such luck. The woman opened the door and asked me what I wanted. I blurted out my crime and handed the evidence to her. She didn't scold as I thought she might, but told me I could have a blossom once in a while if I would ask first. So I asked her if I could have that one back and she said, "No, because you took this without asking. Stop and see me another day."

We all have lessons to learn in life, and learning them is often hard. It's only as we look back years later that we can laugh at ourselves.

The problem is, we're not willing to learn hard lessons. We want everything in life to be easy and life doesn't work that way. If we *won't* learn the hard way, life keeps dumping the same lessons on us again and again in different ways until the "easy" way is harder on us than learning it right the first time.

Learning from Life

Life is a school,
with lessons every day.
Happy the child who learns them
while she may,
And finds, once learned,
they stand her in good stead
To meet the trials of life which lie ahead.

Gleaning

Fall 1997

I've been gleaning. Gleaning is picking up the scraps that others have left behind, and making use of them. It is a practice as old as time.

In Bible times, gleaning meant picking up the bits of fallen grain left behind by the reapers and binders—all hand work in those days. The reapers cut the grain with a sickle and the binders gathered it into bundles and tied it, then stood the bundles together on end to finish drying. Later, the bundles were taken to a threshing floor to separate the grain from the straw and chaff.

Gleaners gathered the scatterings from the field and carried them home in bags or baskets to make flour for baking. The straw they separated from the grain might be used to weave fresh sleeping mats or to start the day's fire for cooking. Gleaners performed a useful service and also helped feed their families.

I've been gleaning. Our son called us a couple of weeks ago and said he'd been harvesting his garden all day, expecting a frost that night. He knew he had more tomatoes than he could possibly use and if we wanted some, we could come help ourselves.

There was a chill breeze as we loaded bags and boxes with tomatoes of all sizes and colors, green, yellow, red, some ripe and some just beginning to turn.

We helped Neil, but we also helped ourselves. First, Tricia and I made green tomato mincemeat. Four batches of it. Enough for pie and cookies for a long time. Then I began turning the ripe tomatoes into chili sauce, the old fashioned kind that is sweet instead of hot.

The smaller green tomatoes became tender, spicy pickles and I even had enough green ones left to make piccalilli. That's another old fashioned recipe for what is called green pickle relish today. But I like the sound of piccalilli; it's a delicious word that recalls the spicy aroma of my mother's kitchen long ago.

I tell you all this because I think gleaning, and the pickling and preserving that often follow it, are almost a forgotten art in our society. And that is too bad. The bright colors of fresh fruits and vegetables, the hard-work togetherness of all the necessary preparations, and the wonderful aromas that fill the house are powerful bonding agents. They help give families a heritage, and a feeling of satisfaction and accomplishment.

Over the years, we've gleaned wild apples from trees grown old and gnarly. Often they are lost varieties not cultivated anymore, and make marvelous cider and flavorful applesauce. We owe a debt of gratitude to whatever "johnny appleseed" planted them, perhaps a century ago. Such a tree grew near our farm house. It was a snow apple tree, not a variety you'll find in the supermarket. Probably you won't even find it at a pick-your-own orchard. Why they were called snow apples, I'm not sure. It could be because they have a very white flesh inside their red and green skin, or because they develop their best flavor after a hard frost or snow.

We've also gleaned butternuts from beneath the tree of a neighbor who already had all she wanted. We even left some for the squirrels to winter on. And we've gleaned the acorns that scatter themselves across our lawn in the fall. The Department of Environmental Conservation buys them for starting new oak trees.

Even ideas can be gleaned. A chance remark, a sudden thought shared, a wise or witty book, all can yield just the right scraps from which to weave a new story or improve a life philosophy or solve a knotty problem.

One friend gleans wildflowers and grasses to make decorative dried flower arrangements. Evergreen cones are a favorite freebie from nature. I have a handsome Christmas wreath made from cones by another friend. It will last for years. Some folks glue small stones together and paint faces on them to create whimsical little animal figures. An old neighbor gleans scraps of wood and carves them into unique Father Christmas figures.

The late Pat O'Brien showed me an unusual necklace he had made from moose pellets dipped in shellac and made into beads. His wife refused to wear it, but it became an interesting conversation piece. He also had made some very attractive porcupine quill jewelry, and others have done the same

Fascinated by the variety of wood grains, I often save scraps others would throw away. Some have pictures in them that come alive with just a little color added. Others inspire poetry. One came from a burl gleaned by the road. Often found with unique grain patterns, burls are like tumors growing on a tree. Some woodworkers make decorative bowls from burl wood. This particular burl was dozy; soft, pithy lines wormed their way through it. But as I looked at it, a thought came to me and grew into a poem. I inscribed it on pieces of that old wood.

This Old Wood

Like this old wood, my life shows stain
    of creeping flaws within the grain.
Yet the Creator looks, and sees
    a thousand possibilities, and
        brings forth beauty from disease.
Like this old wood,
    beneath Love's hand,
        I am transformed in ways not planned.

Flying Lessons

1996

In the fall of 1967, Don bought an airplane. It became the fulfillment of a childhood dream.

"If we wait until the barn is paid for," he said, "the children will be all grown and gone."

It was a used plane, of course, and at that time it cost less than a decent used car does today. It had four seats and was ideal for flying Sunday afternoon sightseers. Over 150 people had their first plane ride in that craft and Don said that although many of them were nervous at first, he never had one who said they wouldn't go again.

Don and a neighbor, John Lepkowski, took ground school training together at MVCC, and we soon got used to hearing the jargon of flight enthusiasts. What we would refer to as a steering wheel was actually the yoke. Turning in the air was called banking. The cowl was what we'd normally think of as a hood; underneath it was the engine compartment. Maps were called charts, and a pre-flight check list was something pilots went through religiously before taking off. *Every time*. It could mean the difference between life and death.

VFR

Keeping track of weather predictions, as farmers all do, Don was soon more involved than ever in his weather watching. If the skies were clear, with ceiling and visibility unlimited, it was a VFR day. That meant Visual Flight Rules could be used, following the chart and maintaining visual contact with landmarks along the way.

VFR flight was beautiful after dark. From a mile or so up in the night sky, we could see the lights of Utica and Watertown, Rome, Carthage, Lowville and all the smaller towns between—all at the same time! In winter, yard lights at farm after farm reflected off the snow, making it easy to see exactly where we were.

VOR

Radio communication skills were a must, no matter what the flight conditions. We learned there is a network of VOR transmitters across the country which are used for radio navigation. By tuning the plane's omni radio to the known frequency of a particular VOR, the pilot can fly directly over it or can chart how many degrees from the transmitter will lead to a given destination.

This all sounds complicated, and at first it is. But once the language is learned and the student puts in some practice time with a good instructor, many of these tasks become almost automatic, like driving a car along a county road where there's very little other traffic.

We've been asked how you keep from colliding with other airplanes in the sky, because there aren't any roads and road markings there to keep travelers apart. But there *are*. They just aren't visible without knowledge of flight rules and an understanding of the instrument panel. Different altitudes are assigned to planes flying in different directions. Instruments indicate altitude, speed and direction of flight, and radio contact with nearby control towers keeps the pilot aware of the position of other planes in the vicinity.

Short of mechanical failure, extreme weather, sudden pilot illness or sabotage, there is almost no likelihood of a midair collision. Such catastrophes happen much more frequently on the ground. In fact, trained pilots insist the most dangerous part of an airplane trip is the drive to the airport.

IFR

Don's plane was a Piper Cherokee 235, formerly an instrument flight trainer. This means it was used to teach pilots how to fly when they don't have VFR conditions. You may have seen planes flying through clouds or heard them go over at night and wondered how the pilots can tell where they are. All those instruments make it possible to adjust airspeed and direction, maintain radio communication, determine exact location and estimated time of arrival at destination. Large airports are equipped not only with control towers and radar, but with sophisticated instrument landing systems (ILS) which enable the pilot to land the plane safely and smoothly even in dense fog.

A very important instrument on the panel is the artificial horizon. This is a round dial with a horizontal line across the middle and the likeness of a small airplane centered on the line. When banking to the left, the plane tilts with the left wing below the line and the right wing above. If the pilot can't see the natural horizon, all it takes is a look at the artificial horizon to determine if the plane has returned to level flight.

This is extremely important if the pilot is disoriented or suffers vertigo. It is possible to *feel* as if the plane is level even when it is not. One of the first things students are taught when learning to fly by instruments is to *trust* those instruments. Feelings are not reliable, especially if the pilot is fatigued, has been doing difficult maneuvers, is short of oxygen or is flying where the horizon is not visible.

Learning to fly safely and successfully is like learning to live safely and successfully. There are rules and regulations to be learned. There are charts to follow and signals to listen for and all kinds of instruments to keep us on course.

Like an airplane, we have a built-in guidance system. We call it a conscience, and it lets us know when we need to make course corrections in our life. If we rely on our feelings, we could be in for all kinds of trouble, just as a pilot would be who ignored his artificial horizon because he felt as if his plane was flying on the level when it wasn't.

The laws of society, family traditions, faith, good habits, school and work schedules, weekly commitments, short and long range goals are some of the instruments that help keep us on course.

Anyone can fly through life when it's clear and sunny. But when fogs of confusion or storms of temptation or the darkness of despair shape our flight conditions, we need to trust our instruments for safe passage. Feelings are not reliable.

Rising on Wings

Life calls me to climb,
Like a homesick angel,
Up to the altitudes
Brimming with light,
Where I can look out
With limitless vision
And see with perspective
The plan of my flight.

Life calls me to soar
Above indecision,
Above the anxieties
Bound in the sod,
And view the perplexities
Humans can conquer
When tuned to the frequency
Some know as GOD.

Labor Saving Devices

Fall 1994

The sound of fall whooshed down our street today—the village vacuum cleaner, its giant hose slurping up windrows of leaves along the curb, chewing them into sudden dust and blowing them into a truck-top bin. I used to grab a rake when I heard that sound and rush out to move more leaves off the lawn. But I know they'll be back; there are plenty of leaves still on the trees, falling lazily one or two at a time, covering the driveway so recently swept.

This summer Don found a leaf blower at a yard sale. In half an hour with that blower he can clear as many leaves off the lawn as I could with a rake in hours. Personally, I don't like the noise it makes but I'm glad to see the work done quickly and I'm glad he has fun doing it. I still sweep driveway and rake around the edges when he's not looking. I enjoy the sunshine, fresh air and exercise, too.

Labor saving devices are wonderful. But they make me wonder about how much labor they really save, and if that saving of labor is always in our best interests.

Take the leaf blower for instance. I love to rake and normally do most of it, so when Don moves leaves, he's *adding* labor for himself even though he's saving me some tired muscles.

Another labor saving device is the bread mixer. This is sort of half way between the old fashioned kneading it by hand and the newfangled dump-the-ingredients-in-and-flick-the-switch automatic bread maker. The mixer is a pail that clamps to the counter and has a large dough hook in it. You put the ingredients in and turn the handle for a few minutes, then let the dough rise. It saves all that hard labor of kneading by hand. On the other hand, I have a friend who takes out her frustrations by kneading bread--better than punching a person. The modern bread maker is handy if you're short on time but like the smell of fresh baked bread. Trouble is, it only makes one loaf at a time, not the eight loaves the bread mixer stirs up. Extra loaves make nice gifts.

Before she went in for surgery, our daughter stocked up on convenience foods—things that could be popped in the oven for a family dinner, with no preparation other than unwrapping. I think that kind of labor saving device is super—if you've just had surgery, or if you have unexpected company drop by just before mealtime. But anyone who loves to cook can tell you that such pre-prepared meals don't taste like homemade, and certainly aren't as much challenge and fun nor as satisfying to culinary creativity.

I tell you all this because I think there is something in the make up of our human nature that is not quite happy unless it has some real work to do. We use dozens of labor saving devices, then go out jogging or pumping iron or riding bike to give our muscles the exercise and stimulation they have been deprived of by our make-life-easier appliances and gadgets.

Kids used to walk great distances to school. Now we send out buses to transport them (at great expense to the taxpayers). This labor saving device robs kids of fresh air and exercise they need for good health. So we build gymnasiums and athletic fields and shower/locker rooms (at great expense to the taxpayers) so the kids can get the exercise they need to stay healthy.

There is another perspective on labor saving devices, too. It is illustrated well by a doctor's comment on farmers. They used to walk behind the plow, he said, and when the horse needed to rest, the farmer rested also. Today, they fuel up the tractor and pound their bodies over those ruts and bumps with almost no rest. Even at night they don't slow down. They work the fields by tractor headlights. The doctor insisted that the old time farmers lasted longer than today's farmers do with all their labor saving devices. Part of the problem is that those labor saving devices cost a lot of money, so farmers often add land to produce more crops or livestock to pay for the new machinery. Talk about vicious circles.

It is a fact that labor saving devices of any kind leave us free to accomplish more in other areas. But it is also a fact that we often stretch ourselves too far, trying to do everything that comes to hand. We have become so *do* oriented that we forget to *be*.

Take Time to BE!

Be kind even though you are busy;
Take time if a friend wants to share
Some hopes, some dreams or some heartaches.
Take time to just listen and care.

Be grateful for all of your blessings.
Be generous, thoughtful and true.
Be patient when someone is trying
Or looking for guidance from you.

And what you must *do*, do it wisely,
But remember, it's better by far
To be known, not so much for your *doing*,
As for what kind of person you are.

Living in Fear

1993

"Not Guilty," the jury said.

The parents of Yoshi Hattori sat in stunned silence as their son's killer was cleared of blame. How could these Japanese parents comprehend what had just happened?

Last fall, their son had stopped at a house to ask directions to a party he'd been invited to in the neighborhood. A man met him at the door with gun in hand and told him not to move. Confused, Yoshi stepped forward to explain his plight and was shot dead, supposedly taken for an intruder.

What has our society come to when innocent people can lose their lives just because they ask for help? Have bizarre movies and television made us so paranoid that we kill strangers with impunity, just because they *might* be planning to harm us? Something is wrong here!

Whatever happened to the ancient custom of hospitality, of lending a helping hand to strangers? Whatever happened to the ancient American principle that a person is innocent until proven guilty? What kind of anguish would we put ourselves through if everyone reacted as that homeowner did?

When we were still on the farm, I woke one night to the sound of the front door opening. All our children were in bed and asleep. An eerie shiver went up my spine. I shook Don to alert him, then went to investigate, quietly, without turning a light on.

When I reached the head of the stairs, I heard footsteps coming up. "Who is it?" I asked. "It's Judy," came a startled voice in reply. She had stopped on her way home from work, sick and needing some comfort and advice on what to do at this time of night. What if I had approached that ominous sound with a gun in my hand? What if I had shot first and asked questions later?

I shudder to think of what I would have had to live with for the rest of my life—a widowed son, two grandchildren that never would have been born, the loss of a loved daughter-in-law and friend, and a feeling of horror that would never go away.

A few years ago, our son-in-law Jeff woke to a similar sound at his front door. He slipped quickly out of bed and headed for the landing above his entryway. "Who's there?" he asked sternly. "It's me, dad," came the voice of his 6-year old son. Jeff snapped on the light. "What are you doing outdoors at this time of night?" he asked incredulously. "I heard it starting to storm and remembered I left the rake outside," explained Benjamin, "so I went out to get it."

Jeff doesn't own a gun. After that experience, I don't think he ever will.

I tell you all this because I think we need to reevaluate our attitudes and priorities. Living in fear is unhealthy not only for the person at the barrel end of the gun, but for the person on the trigger end.

We need to ask ourselves what things are really important to us in life. A trusting, happy family? Doors open to friends and neighbors in need? A quality of friendliness and mercy that gives everyone the courtesy of being heard without pre-judging? Or do we want to live in armed isolation, cringing in fear behind locked doors?

I feel sorry for the young exchange student who couldn't find his way to the party. I feel sorry for the bereaved parents who simply cannot believe or comprehend what happened to their son. I feel sorry for the homeowner who was so paranoid he acted first and thought about it afterwards. I feel sorry for the jury who concluded his reactions had not been improper. And I feel sorry for a society that condones this kind of aberrant behavior. How can we ever cry, “Lord have mercy on us!” if we show no mercy ourselves?

Prayer for Mercy

Give me a tender heart, God,
      and an understanding mind.
“Make me an instrument of Thy Peace.”
      Help me be thoughtful and kind.

Touch with your healing presence
      each hurt,
            and dry each tear.
Fill me with loving kindness
      and take away all fear.

Help me to reach out to others—
      The lonely,
            The frightened,
                  The lost.
Help me to be a friend to all
      And never to count the cost.

Dying in Peace

Author's note: Several years ago, a dear friend shared the following experience with me. I retell it here with her permission, changing minor details to protect her family's privacy. This touching and joyful story fits so well with the theme of this book, it would be a shame not to include it.

* * * * *

I spent over twelve hours a day with my mother-in-law at the hospital during her final stay there. By day 18, at her request, we had revised her living will and stopped all treatment except comfort measures. Desperately ill, she had decided the time for her to go was now. She could see Dad waiting for her near the bed in a silver Mercury convertible, winking at her, and she knew he was there to take her on their final trip together. (He had died several years earlier).

Every time she'd wake again, she'd be angry. "Why am I still here? Why won't God take me? I'm ready. You can do it. You know what to do, you can send me home! Do it. Just do it

This was one angry, bitter, hostile woman who had alienated many people in her lifetime. I finally told her that perhaps God was giving her a chance to make things right with some of her broken relationships before he took her. I asked her to picture someone she'd had a bad relationship with that she'd like to have fixed before she left. She could do that. I then told her to go and talk to them and work it out and come back when it was better.

She seemed to be in a very deep sleep (coma?) for nearly three hours when I noticed tears at the corner of her eye. I brushed them away and she opened her eyes and whispered, "You were right. It was wonderful! Now I'm ready to go." I proceeded to ask her if there was someone else. She shook her head no, so I started naming names. "OK, OK, I'll do it again!" She closed her eyes and was gone again.

This happened with at least six different people, each episode lasting an hour to six hours, over the final three days of her life. Slowly, I watched her personality change. The anger was gone, the harshness dissipated, her frequent petulance, impatience, arrogance, fear....all vanished. In the meantime, Dad stayed close by in that car. So closely that the nurses moved the bed next to hers out of the room so he could park there till she was ready to get into the car.

This determined lady didn't want her sons to see her die. Every time they'd come in the room during the last half day, her breathing and heart rate would normalize, even though she did not seem to be awake. When they left the room for the last time, I spoke into her ear...

"They're gone and won't be back for a half hour. This would be a good time if you're ready to go." Ten minutes later, with a slight smile on her face, she breathed her last.

I tell you all of this because, if I had hastened her dying as she asked me to do on day 18 or day 19, she would not have experienced the mending of relationships that took place on days 20 and 21. And she would not have died with such a sense of peace and rightness.

November Notes

1995

Welcome to November! This is an interesting month in many ways. Originally the ninth month of the year (novem means nine in Latin), November was pushed into its present place when two egotistical Roman emperors, Julius and Augustus Caesar, decided they wanted pleasant summer months named after them.

In our own country, November has seen its share of action in the struggle for equal opportunity for women. On November 1, 1848, the Boston Female Medical School opened its doors to twelve women determined to be doctors. The male medical establishment tried to ignore this "foolishness", and it was years before the school gained widespread respectability when it merged with Boston University in 1874.

November 2, was also an eventful day in our history. On that day in 1795, James K. Polk was born in Pineville, North Carolina, and grew up to become the first "dark horse" presidential candidate. At the Democratic convention in 1844, VanBuren and Cass were the two contenders and seven rounds of voting had already taken place without reaching the required two-thirds majority. A compromise candidate was suggested as a way to break the standstill. Polk's name was added to the mix drawing 44 votes on the eighth ballot. When the ninth ballot was counted, Polk was the party's nominee. He went on to win the election and become our 11th president.

Also born on November 2, was Warren G. Harding, our 29th president. The year was 1865, and his birthplace was Blooming Grove, Ohio. At the time of the 1920 Republican

Convention, the field was crowded with distinguished candidates, with Harding so far down on the list of possibilities he wasn't even seeking the presidency. But a crafty Ohio politician named Harry Daugherty had other ideas. Talking to a reporter, Daugherty predicted the Convention would run into a stalemate.

"After the other candidates have failed," he said, "the leaders, worn out and wishing to do the very best thing, will get together in some smoke-filled hotel room about 2:11 in the morning. Some fifteen men, bleary-eyed from lack of sleep, and perspiring profusely with the excessive heat, will sit down around a big table. I will be with them and present the name of Senator Harding. When that time comes," he said, "Harding will be selected." And that is precisely what happened.

On November 2, 1889, North and South Dakota became the 39th and 40th States. This culminated nearly twenty years of arguing over where the Dakota state capital should be located. The only thing the leaders could agree on was to disagree and so Dakota split into two separate states, each with its own capital.

And in 1920, on November 2, radio station KDKA, Pittsburgh, began the nation's first radio broadcast. The big news of the day—election returns for the first presidential election in which women had the legal right to vote.

Many years earlier, Susan B. Anthony, impatient with ridiculous male supremacy notions, led a march of suffragettes to Rochester's city hall and demanded to be registered to vote. Undaunted by the official refusal to see reason, she cast her ballot anyway, on November 5, 1872!

Politics prevails in early November. And sometimes it takes surprising turns, as the above stories show. Another big surprise came in 1948, when the *Chicago Daily Tribune* published the election results before the final returns were in. So confident were they in the outcome that their banner headline reads: DEWEY DEFEATS TRUMAN. A UPI newsphoto, printed later that same day, shows a grinning president-elect Harry Truman holding up the newspaper with the erroneous headline, inviting the world to laugh with him.

Now the *Chicago Daily Tribune* editors were not the only ones in error that day. History also points a finger at the apathetic Republicans who didn't bother to vote, confident that their candidate, New York's Governor Thomas E. Dewey, would win anyway. Today, you never even hear his name. You only see it on signs along the Thomas E. Dewey Thruway, if you travel that road. And I dare say many who travel it still have no idea who he was. Fame is a fickle mistress.

I tell you all these things to remind you of the importance of voting. When it comes to political issues and candidates, Americans are a noisy and opinionated crowd. But if all we do is *talk*, we cheat ourselves of the chance to pull that lever and make a statement that really counts.

See you at the polls.

* * * * *

If

If rocks could walk, and roads could talk
And a rill could spill out money,
If stars could croon to the rising moon,
O, wouldn't that be funny?
If books could sing and trees take wing,
And sharks should lose their jaws,
And common sense cost two half pence,
I'd tell you this—Because!...

Carpe Diem

1999

November 2, 1999. Go to the polls and vote. Keep that appointment with the dentist. Make plans for Thanksgiving. Think of all the things there are to be thankful for. Water the plants. Make stew. Pray for Wisdom. Visit with a friend over hot tea. Write a letter. Check the birthday and anniversary list. Buy cards. Take the dog for a walk. Dig some more parsnips or rutabagas. Bake cookies. Check the mail, and the e-mail. Pay bills. Read the newspaper. Pray for peace in a world where many know only war and destruction. Lend a hand. Speak a word of encouragement to someone.

Each day carries its own list of things to do. Some of those tasks are mere repetition—eating meals, washing dishes, combing hair. Others are seasonal—putting the lawnmower away, getting the snowblower out, making holiday plans. A few are truly life changing activities—welcoming a new baby, burying a spouse, finally kicking the nicotine habit, hearing from a long lost friend.

The rhythm of these predictables and unpredictables, the mundane and the sacred, the routine and the unexpected, give a texture to our days that keeps us from becoming complacent. If the texture is painful, it makes us more aware of life's truly vital elements. If the texture is soft and smooth, we experience comfort and relaxation. If the texture is electric, we are energized.

I tell you all this because I think we sometimes become mentally lazy and just let life happen to us, when we could take an active part in what happens and in how we choose to respond to events that are beyond our control.

When I started writing this week's column, I checked my Book of Days in American History. The Journal was coming out on November 2nd, so I looked to see what happened on that date. I discovered a truly fascinating person whose birthday is today. He was our nation's eleventh president. All I had known about him before was his name—James K. Polk.

What I discovered in my research was so extensive, so stirring to the imagination, that I decided to turn it into a feature story instead of a column. Here was a man who lived in the middle of controversy, but steadfastly followed the path he thought best for the nation. In that respect, he was very much like Abraham Lincoln, who was one of his detractors at the time.

Polk did not just let life happen to him. He took active steps to improve his mind. He was decisive about things that needed to be done. He did not crave power or prestige, but with humility served his country to the best of his ability.

Thrust into center stage by events not of his making, he became President of the United States without ever seeking the office. He had no multi-million-dollar campaign fund. He had no television coverage. He had no ambitions of becoming president. But an active life of public service had prepared him well for holding that office.

Reading some of his speeches, I couldn't help but wish today's political contenders had as much depth of character as Polk did. Because he served in turbulent times, the political cartoonists had a ball poking fun at him. But he knew what he was about and was not swayed by their satirical humor.

Perhaps today's highschool students should study some of our early presidents, not just to memorize names and dates, but to see what real statesmanship looked like without the lavish window dressing that "enhances" leaders in this electronic age.

They might learn, for instance, that true leadership is not about exchanging political favors. It is not about popularity or good looks. It is not about money. It is not about putting one's personal desires first, but rather asking what is best for the country, and then acting on that.

My column had a slow and uncertain start, as it sometimes does. But it gave me the opportunity to learn something new, to stretch my mind and to revel in the obvious lessons history is ready to teach us if we choose to pay attention.

Seize the Day!

Seize the day. Yes! Grasp it with boldness.
No ordinary day is this. Therefor,
Refuse to settle for the usual. Look, instead,
For the profound that lies hidden in the simple,
For the blessing that pervades the pain,
For sudden calm midst the day's confusions.

Seize the day! Accept the challenge to discover
The stretching of a comfort zone,
The expanding of awareness horizons,
The healthy change of pace that clings
To unplanned interruptions,
The tug of compassion at another's distress.

So full of opportunity—this path we walk,
That we should seize each hour, and make it talk!

Harden Furniture

November 1996

After we voted on Tuesday, Don and I drove to McConnellsville to see the Harden Furniture Company facilities. On our way, we stopped to take our daughter and son-in-law with us for the outing. The tour, arranged by THRIFT for its members and friends, was fascinating and informative.

In the 1840s, three Harden brothers formed a construction company in McConnellsville. Raw materials came from family-owned woodlands. Logs cut there supplied them with dimension stock and lumber for their building projects.

During rainy seasons, or when snow was too deep for working in the woods, the loggers were given indoor work making kitchen chairs from the short-piece remnants not useable in construction. "Waste not, want not," was a maxim of the day and the Hardens didn't waste anything that could be used.

Their kitchen chairs became quite popular. When they finally checked the ledgers to see how well their business was doing, they were surprised to find the chairs were making more money for them than the construction business. It was then they made the decision to go into full time furniture production. They terminated their construction business and expanded their line to include other styles of chairs, tables, bedsteads, cabinets and dressers.

Requests for matching items began coming in from as far away as the west coast. Obviously, Harden Furniture had migrated westward by wagon train with the pioneers. Now that the adventurers were settled in their new homes and established in business, they wanted to complete their furnishings with matching pieces.

Today, Harden Furniture is in demand in all 48 contiguous states and in many foreign countries as well. Harden has its own fleet of trucks which make regular runs to all points of the compass, still delivering high quality furniture from a business now in its fifth generation of family ownership.

The tour begins at the log yard, just beyond the complex of buildings. Here we see pile after pile of cherry logs. Hardens produce cherry furniture almost exclusively, although maple is used for drawer sides and backs and for framing inside the upholstered pieces. Cherry, we learned, is almost white when first sawn but with exposure to light the wood takes on a rosy hue, gradually darkening to a rich reddish brown color.

Inside the first building, the noise level rises dramatically as the sound of the debarking machine and slab saw fill the air. Thin slabs of wood, with inner bark still clinging, are carried by conveyor to an automatic dumping station.

This scrap wood, chopped and moved to one of two huge silos near the plant, comes back to the furnaces, which produce heat for the entire complex. Nothing is wasted. Sawdust, sanding dust and small scraps all follow this efficient recycling route. These by-products, including bark, knots and other blemishes, constitute about two thirds of the volume of each log used.

The remaining log is sawn into lumber and carried by conveyor to other saws, which cut it into pre-determined lengths, sorted by size electronically in this computer-driven, automated operation.

Farther along, human hands and eyes sort and arrange pieces for the most attractive flow of grain patterns in the finished piece. These arrangements are glued together in proper sequence and are clamped for about four hours while the glue bonds the pieces together.

In another area, routers and carvers are at work shaping the wood to fit the design and pattern currently in production. This can change depending on which products have been ordered. Even here, the computer makes decisions as orders are fed in, sometimes for custom built, one-of-a-kind items. At each step of production, attention to detail and careful workmanship are evident, a symbiotic relationship between computers, machinery, humans and trees.

Farther on we see workers assembling components, tying springs expertly, adding padding, cutting and stitching fabrics and applying wood finishes. Back in the showroom area we are free to browse. This section is extensive with room after room full of tastefully arranged china cabinets, dining tables, mirrors, sofas and more.

In the space of two hours, we have seen a spellbinding process carry our imaginations from the 1840s to the present. From logs to lounges, from saws, shapers and sanders to smoothly polished tables and book shelves we have witnessed the transformation of rough materials into carefully crafted works of art and utility.

Naturally, some steps in the process take considerably longer than the two hours we spent. We weren't following a single log through the process. After the log is cut into lumber, the boards are stacked outdoors with small sticks between layers to let the air circulate and partially dry each piece. This may take months before those stacks are moved to dry kilns where even more moisture is removed, bringing the lumber to a standard percentage of moisture.

Life is like that. We start out rough and life tumbles us in a variety of circumstances to wear away the unneeded bark and flaws before the whining saws and planers, routers and sanders of life can shape us into the carefully crafted works of art we are destined to become. Such sanding and polishing usually doesn't feel very good, but it is essential to bring out the grain of our character and the luster of our inner beauty.

Like a Tree

How very like a tree we grow,
so slowly stretching,
year by year,
Up from the soil of ages past,
up through the storms
of doubt and fear.

Then, cut from the stump of family,
and stacked with others
to learn and strive,
We are shaped by forces
we can't control, but slowly discover
we're more alive.

Rude and thoughtless
we entered life, weathered
by wind and rain and sun,
Then, smoothed and polished
by hands unseen,
we find our real life just begun.

Thanksgiving

1995

How many things fill up our days. A good-bye kiss. An early errand run. A good book lent to a friend. A phone call to check on someone who is having problems. A Christmas present delivered ahead of time because *now* is when it's needed. A cup of tea with a neighbor. Planning ahead for Thanksgiving. Shooing the cat off the table. Again. Giving the old dog his medicine. Patching a favorite shirt that is thinning at the elbows. Praying for a friend in the hospital. Unloading the dishwasher. Filling it up again. Watering the impatiens plants, which are blooming brightly, quite unaware that it's snowing outside.

The sacred and the mundane intertwine, threading their way through the hours like embroidery floss embellishing a sampler. Sometimes we end up feeling we've frittered away a whole day doing such little things. More often we feel richly blessed because a friend has confided in us or a grandchild has come to us for comfort or someone has trusted in our wisdom and asked for advice.

This week we celebrate Thanksgiving. I think, really think, about all the little blessings and challenges, disappointments and renewed hopes that give my life texture and meaning. I ponder the many people, places and events that work their magic to make me thankful. They are more than I can number.

I look outside my window to see a light snow falling and I am thankful for a warm house. I look at the cat stretched out napping on the sofa and I am thankful for my vacuum cleaner. I listen to the patient tick of the old clock on the bookcase and I am thankful for those who came before us, for the simple treasures they acquired and passed on.

I feel the keyboard beneath my fingers, translating my thoughts into word pictures, and I am thankful for computers. The telephone rings and I am thankful that I have learned to say no to high-pressure telemarketers. It rings again and I am thankful for a daughter-in-law who is helping me with Thanksgiving arrangements. The dishwasher purrs and swishes in the background and I am thankful for this extra time it gives me to visit with you.

I didn't always have a warm house. I remember when I was growing up, we rented a house that had frost on the insides of the living room walls. We tacked blankets up for insulation and fed more coal to the pot-bellied stove. Another house was so cold we had to run to the stove to warm our hands before we could go back and finish making the bed. The bedroom was so cold our breath hung white in the air and we cuddled together with hot water bottles at our feet in order to be warm enough to sleep at night. Then I was thankful for clean sheets and hot water bottles and a sister to help keep the bed warm.

In those days we didn't have a vacuum cleaner, but a carpet sweeper was much easier and more efficient than using a broom or hauling a heavy rug out to the clothes line to have the dust beaten out of it. We only did that a couple of times a year and we were thankful for the carpet sweeper. And the carpet. It helped keep the floors warm in winter.

Our "dishwasher" was a pair of hands in sudsy water, but we were glad for the companionship of someone else to dry the dishes. We never were bothered by telemarketers. The term hadn't even been invented yet, and if it had, it wouldn't have mattered to us—we didn't have a telephone. Communication was by hand written letter. We didn't have a computer. They hadn't been invented yet, either. We didn't even have a typewriter. Ballpoint pens were yet to appear on the scene. But we found fountain pens were much more convenient than the old dip pens had been.

I tell you all this because I'm convinced our happiness does not depend on what we own. A thankful heart can find something to be grateful for no matter what the circumstances of one's life may be. A thankful heart is as necessary to our emotional and social health as vitamins and minerals are to our physical health. We can get by without them, if we insist, but our quality of life and our enjoyment of life are enhanced by good nutrition *and* by a lifelong habit of thankfulness.

Thanksgiving Acrostic

Take time for gratitude.
Hearts that give thanks
Are happier, far, than
Negative souls and cranks.
Know, without worry or doubt,
Simple joy in sharing
God's openhanded love—
Infinite, patient, caring.
Value the good in all;
In each new day give praise.
Nurture a thankful heart and
God will bless all your days.

No Insignificant People

1995

The date was December 1, 1955. The holiday shopping rush had already started in Montgomery, Alabama, where Rosa lived. She had worked hard at her occupation as a seamstress and had gone shopping for necessities for her family. Laden with bags, she boarded a city bus and sat down to rest her aching feet on the way home.

Rosa had hardly had time to lay her packages down when a man came up and demanded she give him her seat. Now, that made Rosa angry. She figured she had worked just as hard as he had and was just as tired. Probably more so. The fact that he was white and she was black made no difference to her. She was there first. Fair was fair. Rosa refused to move.

The police were called. They arrested Rosa Parks for violating public transportation laws which, at that time and in that place, gave whites priority seating and required blacks to give up their seats if a conveyance was crowded. It took four days for "justice" to be meted out. Rosa was fined $10 for her offence—such humiliating treatment for a tired working woman.

But look at what has happened in the 40 years since then. Those unfair laws, along with many others just as offensive, have been overturned. Rosa may have been an insignificant little nobody in the eyes of the authorities, but her determination triggered a series of actions that have truly benefited society.

* * * * *

It was in early December of the year 1674, that a French explorer in the New World, Jesuit missionary Jacques Marquette, opened a mission house near the shore of Lake Michigan. It was the first building of what was to become a thriving trading post for fur trappers, white explorers and Indians. Marquette could not have imagined, even in his wildest dreams, the great city of Chicago that now stands where he first made a small, brave beginning.

* * * * *

At the time of the Civil War, the process of converting iron into steel was so expensive that widespread use of steel was impossible. But English engineer, Sir Henry Bessemer, was working on that problem. He finally solved it with a new process, which was patented in America on December 5, 1865. His seed idea, backed by perseverance and determination, made possible the hundreds of miles of shining rails that linked the east coast to the west with the transcontinental railroad.

* * * * *

December 6, 1825, President John Quincy Adams gave his First Annual Message to Congress. In this speech, he recommended government support for scientific research, sponsorship of an astronomical observatory, and the establishment of a national university. Those suggestions don't sound foreign to us at all. The government has long been involved in research, exploration and education. But when Congress first heard those ideas, they ridiculed the president and virtually ruined his political reputation. A quiet little man with visionary ideas was written off as a foolish eccentric. But see where his ideas have taken us—beyond the moon and back! They paved the way for advances we merely take for granted today.

* * * * *

I tell you all these things to make a point: Small things and seemingly insignificant people often have a profound effect on the lives of those who follow. The Bible says it this way:

"To shame the wise, God has chosen what the world counts folly, and to shame what is strong, God has chosen what the world counts weakness." (I Corinthians 1:27, New English Version)

When God stepped into human history almost 2000 years ago, he chose the folly of a virgin giving birth. The worldly wise have never accepted that choice. It makes no sense to them. Nor did it make sense for the Son of God, the Savior of humankind, the King of the Universe, to be born in a stable like a common peasant.

God didn't go to the Jewish High Priest to announce the birth of his son; He sent his angels to tell a group of rugged shepherds in the hills above Bethlehem. God didn't go to the political leaders in Jerusalem to tell them a king was born; He sent a star to guide foreigners to the place where the baby was.

God didn't choose the seat of the mighty Roman Empire for the birthplace of the Messiah. He chose an insignificant village in the hills of Judea, a provincial little outpost kept in line by an army of occupation. He didn't choose a doctor, lawyer, minister, concert pianist or sports hero to raise his son; He chose a common laborer, a carpenter.

The worldly wise and politically strong of the 1990s, even in this "one nation, under God," still don't get it. They still think life is about power and prestige, about money and manipulation, about savvy and success. They forget that every time they write a date on a check they are paying homage to that obscure Jewish baby whose coming changed history so much that we measure time by it. B.C.= Before

Christ; A.D.= Anno Domini, which translated means in the year of our Lord.

As we enter Advent, we are surrounded by the sights and sounds of Christmas celebration. Perky little pep-rally bumper stickers remind us that "Jesus is the Reason for the Season." Even so, he is often lost in the rush to get all the shopping done, the gifts wrapped, the tree decorated, the goodies baked, the guest lists checked, the Christmas cards written, the menus planned, the parties gotten ready for.

Now is the time to remember: In God's eyes, there are *no* insignificant people, no unimportant occupations, no prayers too small to be heard, no gifts unworthy if they come from the heart.

Advent

Season of hope...abiding hope
That God will find us true,
Faithfully going about the work
He has given us all to do.

Season of joy...unmeasured joy
That grows in a heart of love
And overflows...
 Like a river of life
Poured out from the Lord above.

Season of expectation...
What will our Christmas bring?
Expensive gadgets
 beneath the tree?
Or a touch...
 from the infant king?

Miracles

2003

Wednesday, November 19th, Jeff and Jean Balch celebrated their 25th wedding anniversary in West Kingston, Rhode Island.

Tuesday, November 25th, Steve and Tricia Kennison, Lowville, celebrated their 25th wedding anniversary.

Tuesday, November 25th, during the Senior Superlatives assembly at LACS, Shawna Colton, Castorland, was honored by her classmates as the senior with the nicest smile.

Wednesday, November 26th, Cherie Binns of Wakefield, Rhode Island, received her International Certification in Multiple Sclerosis Nursing.

Friday, November 28th, Hazel Woodward of Pine Plains celebrated her birthday. Her son-in-law and daughter, Ron and Mary McGlashan, flew in from California and took her out to dinner.

Sunday morning, November 30th, Caroline Suitter delivered her first baby at Glens Falls Hospital and named him Tyler Jeffrey.

Sunday morning, November 30th, Lin Sawyer—Talcottville and her daughter Brandy Ortman—Syracuse, had brunch at Charlie Brown's Bistro near Boonville with other family members. Then the rest of the family went home to the farm while Lin and Brandy drove to Rhode Island.

Monday morning, at Rhode Island Hospital in Providence, Lin donated a kidney to Jeff Balch.

“It’s no big deal,” she said. “He needs a kidney, and I have one to spare.”

Monday morning, Neil Colton took a misstep getting off a ladder and felt his knee pop. x-rays showed a lengthwise fracture to his shin bone and a break inside his knee. Neil already had crutches from previous mishaps, and a daughter to drive him to the hospital. Despite the pain and swelling, no bones were out of place.

These seemingly unrelated incidents have some common threads. All the people involved are members of our family. Jean, Tricia, Cherie, and Lin are our daughters, Shawna and Brandy our granddaughters; Hazel is Don’s aunt; Jeff is our son-in-law; Caroline is Jeff and Jean’s daughter; Neil is our son.

All these happenings are typical of life’s ups and downs. The difficult and painful events teach us to appreciate, even more, the blessings of our particular circumstances, our joy-filled events, families, friends and faith. The news items above are among other birthdays of children, grandchildren and brothers, which occurred in the same time frame. Set in the midst of it all, appropriately, was Thanksgiving Day.

In addition, all of these incidents have elements of the miraculous hidden in them. I pity the unfortunate and the misled, who don’t believe in such things. Miracles are the leaven that makes the loaf of life rise from a shapeless mass into a sweet smelling offering that nourishes others.

Consider the miracle that is life itself—a tiny cell that could scarcely be seen without a microscope—a speck that grows over a nine-month span of time into a complex and unique human being! It is incomprehensible. And yet it happens, day after day, year after year, all over the world.

Give some thought to the miracle of a smile. Shawna was born 21 years ago with multiple handicaps and a prediction from her doctors that she probably would not live to see her first birthday. She gets around with walker and braces or a wheelchair. Her smile is marred, physically, by teeth broken in a fall, and by gums enlarged from the effects of anti-seizure drugs. But her smile is genuine, warm and cheerful—a miracle in itself, given her physical and mental disabilities.

Contemplate the miracle of a single individual living in three different centuries! Impossible? Not at all. Hazel Woodward was born in 1899; in this year of 2003, she celebrated her 104th birthday! She was married for 78 years before being widowed and still lives alone in her own home, checked on often by family and neighbors. She is blessed with reasonably good health and mental clarity,

Celebrate the miracle of marriages that do not fail, but stand the test of time.

And note the miracle of career successes attained after the half-century mark, and earned in spite of adverse circumstances. Multiple Sclerosis is a dreaded disease. It is difficult to diagnose and there is no known cure. Cherie has been its victim for decades, with recurring episodes of disability and periods of remission.

Early on, she found she had to discover all she could about the disease, because most doctors knew so little. She researched advances in MS diagnosis and treatment, and journaled her own experiences. The certification she has earned, rewards her focus and persistence. She is now officially recognized as an expert, both from her studies and her experience. She participates in an online support group for MS patients, and is a consultant for a major pharmaceutical firm.

Think about the miracles of medical science—that were little more than science fiction fantasy a mere century ago—where doctors can remove an organ from a living person and transplant it to the body of another person and have it begin working almost immediately! A liter's output in the first hour is surely a miracle to someone who has been tied to dialysis three times a week for months and months.

Meditate on the miracle of healing. An injured body, treated carefully, will replace damaged tissue over time and become whole again. A broken bone lets marrow seep out to form a callus that strengthens the area, and within weeks the injured part is well.

Ponder, also, the miracle of altruism—the innate ability of human beings to give of themselves for the good of others. Truly, we are made in the image of the Divine! And ponder the miracle of inner peace in the midst of all these life-changing events. What a way to begin Advent, the church's reenactment of the coming of the Prince of Peace.

Our lives may seem mundane at times, but look around you. Miracles are everywhere. This is a tremendous age in which to be alive. This is surely the age of Emmanuel—God with us! A sane brain cannot help but be filled with awe and gratitude.

May your holidays—holy days—be truly blessed.

Conversation with Jesus

December 2001

Jesus, it will be your "birthday" in less than two weeks and we're busy getting ready for the big celebration. But sometimes we wonder how YOU would like to see it done. With the actual date of your birth lost to us in the mists of legend, we've set it at the darkest time of the year. Does that seem strange to you? Or do you think the date is not what's really important?

Your baby pictures are adorable, and we send them to each other in colorful greeting cards, but they're not very much like the dark, smelly barn where you were born. We've cleaned it up and lit it up and sanitized it to the point where you wouldn't even recognize it, except that you are God, and you are tolerant of our foibles.

Sometimes we wonder if you'd rather have us think about the fact that you are here with us, now? Would you be happier if we celebrated *your presence*, instead or *our presents*? How do we sort out the authentic from the artificial? How do we get in touch with the reality of You, amid all this glitter?

Teach us, Lord, how to withdraw from the hurry and bustle of preparations and obligations, decorations and communications. Help us learn how to be still in your presence so that you can speak to our hearts, assuring us that we truly are loved by you. How we wish we could slow down enough to soak up that truth, to feel a joy so deep there will be no words to express it adequately.

We are reminded of Martha, dear Martha, who so wanted to fix a lovely dinner for you, her honored guest. She bustled about the kitchen, tending to many details, getting all hot and bothered because Mary wasn't there helping her. Martha was so wrapped up in the tasks at hand that she was actually neglecting you, even though she thought she was honoring you.

How like Martha we are. We are busy planning a fancy banquet, dressing up our houses, checking to see that we haven't forgotten anything, getting short tempered because we can't be three people at once to handle all the "demands". The demands, of course, are ones we put on ourselves. We don't stop to think that our expectations are not the same as your expectations. But in our resolve to get things right, we often neglect you, too, just like Martha did. She only came to talk to you when she wanted you to chide Mary for not helping. Often, we come to talk with you only when we have something to complain about or to ask you for.

You would have loved to have Martha sit down and enjoy your company as Mary was doing, but Martha was so driven by self-imposed duties that such a choice never even occurred to her. And here we are, no smarter than Martha was, driven by our own self-imposed duties and trying to do more than you designed us to be doing. It is no wonder we become irritable and tired and resentful, just as she did.

Speak to us, Lord, gently, the way you spoke to Martha. Convince us that all this outward show is not really what you are looking for. You just want us to come spend some time with you. Why can't we understand? Why can't we believe it and actually sit down and listen for awhile?

* * * * *

Well, here we are, Lord...we've finally managed to make some time. Now, what do you want to tell us?

What? You want us just to relax for a few minutes?! With company coming in a few days? And the refrigerator needs cleaning. And the laundry hamper is getting full—we should be doing a load right now. And we still don't know what we're going to fix for supper. How can we just relax?

Really? You want us to read your Love Letter to us? What love letter?

Oh, you mean The Bible. Well, we do read it. Sometimes. A little here and there, you know. It's too long to read all at once.

Sorry, we didn't mean to complain. It's really a very nice letter, at least what we can remember of it—all that good stuff about what love means, and how we should love each other. We're sure you must know that last part is not always easy. Did you notice what our neighbor did just the other...

What? You don't want us to complain about our neighbors? Not even about our brothers? Or our sisters? Don't you realize what they're like?

Oops! Sorry again. Guess you know even better than we do what they're like. Guess you know what we're like, too...even better than we know ourselves. Bet you think we'll never get it right. Sometimes we feel that way, too, as if we'll never get it right. As if we'll never be able to please you.

What was it you wanted to show us in your love letter? Oh, yes, we recall that part. It says, "Be still...and KNOW...that I am God."

Oh, we've always known that you were God. Well, almost always; there were a few times we questioned if you were just a pretty story—you know, like Santa Claus and the Easter Bunny and the Tooth Fairy. But *they* never did anything really BIG, like making the whole world and all the stars and clouds and butterflies like you did. Of course we know you're God...but maybe we don't always know exactly what that means.

We missed what part? Oh, the first two words..."Be still." I guess we did. Here we've been chattering all this time and have hardly given you a chance to talk at all. O.K., we'll be still for awhile. You just let us know how long, but remember, we've got tons of stuff to get done in the next few days...

* * * * *

(breathe in, breathe out,...breathe in, breathe out, ...breathe in...breathe out...)

This is just like the teacher used to tell us in kindergarten when we couldn't settle for our rest period. In no time we were relaxing and feeling a little sleepy. I remember, we always felt refreshed after our "nap". Breathe in...breathe out...and as we listen to the pattern of our breathing, the words of an old hymn come to mind...

"Breathe on me, Breath of God. Fill me with life anew, that I may love as Thou dost love, and do what Thou wouldst do. Breathe on me Breath of God, until my heart is pure, until with Thee I will one will, to do and to endure. Breathe on me Breath of God, till I am wholly Thine, until this earthly part of me glows with Thy fire divine."

* * * * *

Oh, Spirit of Goodness and Love! That's what you meant when you told us to be still. We don't *have* to "get it right." We don't have to perform, or measure up, or make a good impression. All we have to do is be still, and let You breathe on us. Thank you for showing us this deep and hidden truth. We feel so much better now, so relaxed, not uptight about schedules any more. What a relief. What a re-life!

Because you touched us with your presence, we can face the tasks ahead with confidence. They are no longer our masters. YOU are. And what a gentle Master and how wise. Remind us, Lord, whenever we need reminding, to take some time to sit quietly with you, to drink in your wisdom, to breathe your refreshing presence, and to let you touch our hearts with your love. Happy Birthday, Jesus!

My Gift List

1996

"Got your Christmas shopping all done yet?"

This question was in the air even before Thanksgiving. I just shrug my shoulders and look highly doubtful when I hear it. How does one answer such a question? Is anyone ever really finished? If you're like me, you can always think of something else you wanted to do, someone else you'd like to give a little something to. Nothing is ever really finished the way I'd like it to be.

All year long I do Christmas shopping. I may see something in a catalog that would be just perfect for someone I know. So I send for it and stash it away in a drawer or closet. Maybe the gift I find is at a garage sale or an antique book store. It doesn't matter where it comes from if you know it will please the one who receives it.

I once found an elegant set of stemmed glassware at a yard sale and only spent $2.00 on it. A daughter and son-in-law were delighted with it. At a used book store I found a story of the Sawyer family in New Hampshire. My Sawyer son-in-law has relatives in that region of the country. He loves to read and the discovery of that book was a serendipity. He didn't care that I hadn't bucked the mall crowds to buy his present.

I even go "shopping" among my own possessions, deciding which treasures I'm ready to part with. These become special Christmas gifts for my grown children who have shown interest in them.

I think of the lovely opal ring that had been my mother's. It was a gold band set with five oval blue stones. Its small cardboard box was coming apart. Carefully I taped it together and wrote a little note telling what I knew of its origin. Wrapped in white tissue paper and tied with a tiny red bow, the package became a Christmas decoration in one of my shelf displays. A card on the tree told my daughter where to look for her present. When she opened it, tears came to the eyes of both of us.

My mother's lavender-scented sachet locket, an embossed silver pendant shaped like a tiny book, went to another daughter. She hugged me long and hard. "You don't know how much this means to me," she said.

This year, with Christmas preparations in full swing around me, I have to stop and sort. "Shopping" is a quiet time for me. I go to my closets and drawers, my secret caches of "things for Christmas", and bring all the boxed and bagged goodies out to the dining room table, which already has had leaves added for company over the Thanksgiving weekend.

I make a lengthy list of all the people I want to give gifts to. Don always goes at the top of the list but I never write down what I'm giving him, because he'll be going over the list with me later to help fill in with gift suggestions for those not yet covered by my squirreling-away method.

Seven children and their spouses are on the list, all treasured in our hearts and all remembered with something special at Christmas. And there are nineteen grandchildren to bless, four of them in college already. A step-grandson is grown and gone. We don't hear from him, but will think of him with fondness and good wishes.

Special friends and extended family members also show up on our Christmas list from time to time. They don't expect anything in the line of presents, but surprises are such fun. I have a cousin who loves my candied grapefruit peel. There'll be some waiting for her. Our sisters and brothers have their own family circles and limited means, but occasionally we come across something we know would hit the spot for one of them and their name goes on the list.

Last year, I made a collection of *Roundabout* columns I'd written for the holiday season during the past five years. I took it to a local copy shop and had some made for Christmas presents. A distant friend, who reads the column weekly, heard about the project and asked if I might have an extra copy she could buy. I did. Next time she was in town, she came to get it and we had a nice visit, a bonus for both of us.

Yesterday I brought out the hoard of items squirreled away during the past several months. It's time to make my list and sort the treasures, wrap them in festive papers and tag them for identification. Family members who happen in during this process have strict orders not to disturb what is spread out there, and not to be too curious. Surprises are still part of the game.

And yet, amid all these preparations and celebrations, I stop to think about the extravagance of what I am doing. Even though I may not spend a lot of money, I know I am richer in possessions than half the people of the world. While I plan menus and buy food for expected company, I know millions will go to bed hungry on Christmas, and millions will not even know it is a special day, or why it is.

What can I do for them? How can I share my blessings in a way that will enrich their lives? They, too, are my brothers and sisters, my parents and children, my extended family.

Logic tells me I cannot help them all. Compassion tells me I need to help in whatever ways I can. And so I add to my gift list. I add my church's Christmas Joy Offering. Together with the gifts of other church members, this will help support emergency aid for ministers and their families and it will finance college educations for disadvantaged young people.

My check book comes out and I send a gift to Food for the Hungry, one of the most effective non-denominational relief agencies, to help those who would otherwise be physically hungry. I send a gift to the International Bible Society to help feed the spiritual hunger in people's lives. I send a gift to Habitat for Humanity to help provide decent shelter, and to Project Hope for its medical education and assistance programs.

On the other end, each of these gifts is dispensed with the personal touch, the most important ingredient in any gift to anyone at any time of year. And that is why, when I sort out my gifts for others and wrap them in colorful paper, I don't count their dollar value. They are, after all, but symbols of my regard and tokens of my affection. The real gift is myself.

God's Gift List

God made a list for Christmas
    before ever there was such a day.
God gifted us with snowflakes and flowers along our way.
The dark, God filled with glistening stars,
    in day, blue skies above,
With sun and rain and the wind's refrain,
    so we might know of Love.

God set a shining rainbow between the calm and storm,
Then made the wood and oil and coal
    to keep us snug and warm.
God set the birds a singing to welcome each new day,
Then painted evening sunsets in splendored, grand array.

But something yet was lacking in God's celestial plan,
A way to touch earth's people, each woman, child and man.
God looked among the presents still waiting on the shelf,
But none was good enough, so God said, "I will give myself."

And that's how Christmas came to be...
God came to earth, a child like me.

Would you rather be...?

1999

I've noticed several bumper stickers that seem to belong to unhappy people. "I'd rather be fishing" one says. Another declares, "I'd rather be sailing." "I'd rather be flying," says yet another. It seems there are many things people would rather be doing, than what they actually are doing.

In one sense, the bumper stickers are cute and catchy. In another sense, they indicate a large number of people who are dissatisfied with what they are doing. I had a family doctor once who looked out the window longingly, before turning attention to me, then said, "I'd rather be hilling potatoes."

It is a sad commentary on our civilization when people feel forced to do one thing, presumably to earn a living, when they'd really rather be doing something else. Often, the things they'd rather be doing, are probably good indicators of what their secret dreams in life are. I think we all have such dreams. When I was raising children, I sometimes said, "I'd rather be writing." Maybe these longings are meant to steer us in the right direction. A little playtime may help. Let's see.

Back in the '70s, pop psychology games were in vogue. If you attended any kind of business, educational or religious seminar or workshop, you would likely be introduced to one of these games as an "ice breaker", a way for group members to become acquainted.

One such game I remember was "Would you rather be...?" Group members were asked to go to designated areas in the room depending on their individual answer to a given question. For instance, would you rather be a window or a door? All "windows" went to one spot and discussed their reasons for choosing to be windows, while all "doors" went to another spot and discussed why they'd rather be doors. These exchanges of information not only helped participants become acquainted, they often helped individuals develop a clearer understanding of their own thought processes and feelings.

I remember being involved in such a game when the question was posed, would you rather be vanilla ice cream or chocolate swirl nut crunch ice cream? Notice, the question said would you rather *be*, not would you rather *eat*. There were about twenty of us in the group and only two of us chose to be vanilla. I was one of them. The other was a soft-spoken gentleman I'd never met before.

My partner in the vanilla corner said he would rather be predictable and unobtrusive in life than to be the center of attention. That made sense to me. It was a little like vanilla ice cream that is used as the basis for a make-it-yourself sundae. The toppings and decorations get all the attention, but the vanilla ice cream provides the unobtrusive foundation for the resulting fancy dessert.

Chocolate swirl nut crunch ice cream, on the other hand, can lose its appeal fairly rapidly. It can quickly become too much of a good thing, sickishly sweet. Enough, already! I'd rather be the unnoticed support behind the scenes in a project than to be the up-front person who gets all the accolades. I'd rather sit quietly and share my thoughts with you in a weekly "letter" I call *Roundabout*, than to get up and give a speech in public. I'd rather be a simple friend whose encouragement and support help others to shine. In short, I tend to favor being "vanilla".

It is probably no accident that I also prefer vanilla ice cream more often than not. It has that pleasant predictability that can be dressed up with fancy toppings if I'm in the mood for such, but simply can be enjoyed if I want it plain.

Visiting at a daughter's house last week, I chose vanilla ice cream when several dessert selections were offered. My seventeen-year-old granddaughter challenged my choice. "If you're such a fascinating person, how can you prefer plain old vanilla?" she wanted to know.

Now I must confess, I have let my grandchildren know that I am, indeed, a fascinating person. This is not egotism at work; it is merely common sense. I am firmly convinced that any person who reaches "this side of 60" has lived through enough and seen enough of life to qualify as fascinating to the young and inexperienced.

If there are questions they'd like to ask about how it used to be when I was young, or how I feel or what I think about something, now is the time to ask, while I'm still here to fascinate them with my responses. All too often we hear people say, "If only I had listened when my aunt was telling me stories about her adventures," or, "If only my dad were still alive and I could ask him..."

I don't want my grandchildren to be left with such regrets after we're gone, and so I tell them we're fascinating. And I quietly sit here and type my experiences into a column, week after week, most of which are not even read by my grandchildren. Ah, but after I am gone, and they wish they could ask my opinion or advice on something, all they will have to do is look back on the heritage of the written page to figure out what I would say to them. I will never truly be dead to them, because I will always be available through this legacy of "letters".

That pop-psych game of the '70s had another question I remember. Would you rather be a one-room log cabin, or a hundred-room castle? Easy answer for me. I'd rather be the castle, with room for all my children and grandchildren and all their friends to visit and explore and enjoy. I don't want to harbor a lonely hermit. I want to welcome a happy horde.

You'll notice I didn't say I wanted to clean and maintain a hundred-room castle. I'm sure a one-room log cabin would be more equal to my inclination in that way. But games like this are not only fun, they are useful for making us think, not just give the first answer that pops into our mind.

Take—would you rather be a window or a door?—for instance. Some said they'd rather be a door to keep the family safe from bad weather and intruders, who might break a window. Others said they'd like to be a door because doors can swing open and welcome people in, where windows can only let others look in but still be outside. The would-be "windows" said they'd like to let light in and open up vistas of beauty beyond for those inside. Others saw windows as a way of keeping mosquitoes out, while doors that are opening and closing, let insects into the house.

You will notice in these rationales, the players often told more about their own attitudes than about actual windows and doors. That's part of what makes the games interesting. They help us to look at ourselves from different angles and analyze why we think and act the way we do.

Try asking yourself these questions. You may be surprised at the answers and the reasons you come up with. There are no right or wrong answers, of course. You are who you are—unique and valuable. The insights you gain from playing this game will also be unique and valuable. Would you rather be a window or a door? Would you rather be a fountain or a pond? Would you rather be a woodland path or a city street? Would you rather be a Shakespearean sonnet or a newspaper headline? Would you rather be a platinum album hit or a homemade lullaby? Why?

Have fun!

Learn something new.

Share with others.

Live long and prosper!

After-Word

September 2005

I sincerely hope you have enjoyed reading this book, and that it has made you think beyond where you would normally go. If so, it has accomplished its mission.

If you like what you've read, please do me a favor and recommend the book to a friend. My greatest reward will come when some of my readers are inspired to write books based on their own thoughts and experiences. I would love to hear about it if you do.

Additional copies may be obtained directly from the publisher. Order online at www.buybooksontheweb.com or by phone, toll free at 877-BUY-BOOK. You'll find they make much-appreciated gifts for all occasions. Discounts are available in quantity.

Are we at the end already? Before I close, let me leave you with one more reason-rhyme:

Because

Because you've found your way through all these pages
And come, at last, to ask the reason why
I've told you all these tales of fools and sages,
And thoughts you may consider, e'er you die,
I'll now divulge the "why" of my endeavors,
The Reason, is as clear as clear can be—
The more we understand each other's thinking,
    The better world we'll have.
        Don't you agree?

BMC

CPSIA information can be obtained
at www.ICGtesting.com
Printed in the USA
FFOW01n1844151215
19297FF

9 780741 42908